中国传统文化掌上行

唐红梅　著

中国纺织出版社

图书在版编目（CIP）数据

中国传统文化掌上行 / 唐红梅著 . -- 北京 : 中国纺织出版社，2018.7
ISBN 978-7-5180-3966-1

Ⅰ . ①中… Ⅱ . ①唐… Ⅲ . ①中华文化－对外汉语教学－教学参考资料 Ⅳ . ① K203

中国版本图书馆 CIP 数据核字（2017）第 208156 号

责任编辑：汤　浩　　**责任印制**：储志伟

中国纺织出版社出版发行
地　　址：北京市朝阳区百子湾东里 A407 号楼　**邮政编码**：100124
销售电话：010-67004422　　**传真**：010-87155801
http://www.c-textilep.com
E-mail:faxing@c-textilep.com
中国纺织出版社天猫旗舰店
官方微博 http://www.weibo.com/2119887771
北京虎彩文化传播有限公司　各地新华书店经销
2018年7月第 1 版第 1 次印刷
开　　本：880×1230　1/32　**印张**：5.5
字　　数：140 千字　**定价**：49.5 元

前　言

《国家中长期教育改革和发展规划纲要(2010-2020年)》提出，大学教育的培养目标是“培养大批具有国际视野、通晓国际规则、能够参与国际事务与国际竞争的国际化人才”，大学通识教育的核心是提升大学生的文化内涵和素养。大学英语四、六级考试题型也随着纲要的提出而进行了改革。中国传统文化的学习，尤其是翻译，成为大学英语课程侧重的教学内容。加强中西方文化的相互渗透和传统文化解读，从语言学习的角度而言，有利于帮助学生了解目的语和母语的文化差异，提高学生的跨文化交际能力，增强学生的人文知识修养，激发学生的语言学习热情；从考试的角度来看，有利于学生的备考，提升学生的考试成绩。

语言学习的目标就是运用所学到实际的交流中，发表观点，并传播文化。了解中国传统文化源远流长的历史和博大精深的内容，并学习用英语进行表达和交流，可以让学生进一步体验并感受民族文化，学会尊重本民族文化的价值，增强对民族文化的自豪感。同时通过对目的语和母语文化的对比，让学生感受不同文化的精彩，了解文化的多样性，以正确的态度对待文化差异，学会尊重其他民族文化，并能够以平等的姿态、开放的胸怀以及国际视野与其他民族和国家的人民友好交往。

翻译，尤其是笔译，是一项复杂的语言产出过程，需要扎实的基本功。翻译能力的提高需要一定的语法、句法知识、词汇的积累以及驾驭语言的能力。因此，我们在本书的第一章就编入了“翻译与翻译技巧”，在汉语和英语之间如何进行有效转换、如何运用直译法、意译法、转译法、增词法、减词法、反译法等做了较全面的、精确到位的指导，使大学生和英语爱好者对汉英互译有个清晰的认识，举一反三，帮助他们掌握基本的翻译方法，提高翻译水平，对提高考试成绩亦大有裨益。

依据《国家中长期教育改革和发展规划纲要（2010-2020年）》提出的培养目标和现行新大学英语四、六级考试大纲的要求，我们编写了这个适应实际需要、携带方便的中国传统文化小册子。本书选取了一些具有代表性的中国传统文化要点，分为九个类别，以英汉双语做了通俗易懂的介绍。遵循语言学习输入与输出相结合的规律，本书的每一小节都包含了简介、词汇、文化精选、翻译练习和练习参考译文五个部分。本书适用于在校大学生和广大英语爱好者，也适用于对中国传统文化抱有兴趣且具备一定汉语阅读能力的外国读者。我们相信本书对提高文化素养、英语运用水平和沟通能力以及通过其他各类英语考试也有所助益。

编　者

2017年1月

目　录

第一章　翻译和常见的翻译方法

Translation and common translation methods

一、翻译简介

翻译是用一种语言把另一种语言所表达的内容、形式和风格，忠实、流畅而又不乏艺术地再现出来的（言语和思维活动）过程。通俗来说，就是要使原文的内容、风格、韵味在译文中得以再现。鲁迅先生说过：凡是翻译，必须兼顾两面，一则力求其易解，一则是保存着原作的丰姿。

试看以下示例：

例 1：

Studies serve for delight, for ornament, and for ability. Their chief use for delight, is in privateness and retiring; for ornament, is in discourse; and for ability, is in the judgment, and disposition of business.

译文：读书足以怡情，足以博彩，足以长才。其怡情也，最见于独处幽居之时；其博彩也，最见于高谈阔论之中；其长才也，最见于处世判事之际。

译文在内容和形式上都很好地保留了原文的特色，语言精练、优美传神。

例 2：

…and that government of the people, by the people, for the people, shall not perish from the earth.

译文：……民有、民治、民享的政府永世长存。

译文中的“民有、民治、民享”，在形式上对应原文的三个介词词组，在意义上表达精准简明。

综上，翻译既是语义的转换过程，也是语言形式的转换过程。语义转换是翻译的第一追求和最基本的目的，是译者必须达到的标准；而语言形式的转换则是翻译的更高层次的追求，也是区分译文优劣的关键尺度。

二、翻译的标准

现时通用的翻译标准是要兼顾“忠实和通顺”。忠实，既是指对源语内容的忠实，兼指对源语的形式与风格的忠实。而通顺，则是指译文要尊重译语的语言规律和表达习惯。请看以下汉英互译的比较：

例 3：

关关雎鸠，在河之洲。

译文一：Fish hawks cry on the island.（译文只达到了“忠实与通顺”的最基本要求，但忽略了原文的语言形式和特点——拟

声词“关关”的翻译）

译文二：Guan-Guan go the ospreys, on the islet in the river.（形象生动而忠于原文内容和形式）

例 4：

When the radiant energy of the sun falls on the earth, it is changed into heat energy, and the earth is warmed.

译文一：当太阳能到达地球表面时，它就会被转化为热能，然后地球就被加热了。（措辞烦冗，拘泥于原文的语言形式）

译文二：太阳的辐射能到达地球后就转化为热能，从而使大地暖和起来。（忠实通顺，符合行文规范）

需注意的是，在翻译的两个标准中，“通顺”相对容易，而“忠实”则无绝对或完全之说。其一，语言之间是不能画等号的；其二，语言所负载的文化信息也普遍存在不对等的现象。因此，翻译家朱光潜认为绝对的“信”（忠实）“只是一个理想，事实上很难做到”。学者林语堂则说：“译者所能谋达到之忠实，即比较忠实之谓，非绝对忠实之谓。”但除了“极端”的情况之外，“忠实”仍是可以努力实现的。

三、英汉语言对比概述

英汉互译的一切翻译理论、方法和技巧都建立在英汉两种语言的对比上，因此对于翻译实践来说，对比英汉两种语言的异同，尤其是相异之处，从而掌握它们的特点是十分重要的。通过对比，掌握两种语言的特点，有助于在翻译时对译语的把握，做到忠实、通顺达意，同时保持原文的形式和风格。

1. 形合与意合

英语是形合语言，语法规则呈显性，规则先于意义，无规则即无意义。汉语是意合语言，语法规则呈隐性，“意达而已矣”，不苛求非要把语法规则和语言逻辑呈现在明处。

例 5：

英语：It rained so heavily last night.（有主语）

汉语：昨晚下了好大的雨。（无主语）

例 6：

英语：He put his hand into his pocket and brought out his wallet.（有代词指称）

汉语：他伸手从裤兜里把钱包掏了出来。（无代词指称）

2. 词形与词性

英语通过词的形式确定其词性。汉语词没有那么多形式变化，也无从通过词形来判断词性。汉语的词性是由语序来确定的，单讲一个汉语的词，它的词性具有不确定性。

英语：

He received a surprising present from his dad.（动词）

Radio receiver was invented earlier than TV set.（名词）

The ceremony was held in a well-arranged reception room.（名词）

Her mind was extraordinarily receptive.（形容词）

汉语：

在第一季度，中国进口了大量煤炭。(动词)

贸易总额指的是进口与出口的和。(名词)

贸易公司必须申请进口许可。(形容词)

3. 主动与被动

英语被动句多，汉语则主动句多。在汉语中，被动意思常用主动句来表达，少数则使用“经”“受”“遭”“给”“让”“由”等结构来表达。时文“被”字连篇，其实多为西化，并非纯粹的汉语句子。

例 7：

I had my watch repaired today.

我今天让人把手表修好了。

例 8：

Four were killed in the accident.

事故中有四人遇难。

例 9：

He was completely astonished at the news.

这个消息让他大吃一惊。

4. 长句与短句

英语从句多，汉语分句多。英语句子以结构和逻辑为基础，可以在一个主句上衍生多个从句，而且从句也可类似地衍生次级从句，形成一干多枝的结构，理论上可以无限长。而汉语句子以意义为中心，传统上以短句为主。一层意思表达出来，句子即自然地作一停顿；一个意思表达完整，句子就自然结束。即使现代汉语书面语可以把句子写得很长，但中间常用标点分开，事实上还是以小分句为主。

例 10：

英语：I had a kind and patient teacher who often praised all of the students.

汉语：我有一位和蔼耐心的老师，（他）经常表扬我们。

此例中，英语句子结构为一主一从，从句以定语的形式依附于主句。而汉译句子则在原文主从句结合处断开，处理为两个小分句的形式。

例 11：

英语：We have come to dedicate a portion of that field, as a final resting place for those who here gave their lives that that nation might live.

汉语：为使这个国家能够生存下去，烈士们献出了自己的生命；我们来到这里，是要把这个战场的一部分奉献给他们，作为最后的安息之所。

此例中，原文有三层主从句子结构，从形式上看，一句一逗，两部分。译文则把原文中的定语从句 who here gave their lives that that nation might live 及其辖下的目的状语从句 (so) that that nation might live 单拿出来，作为分句处理。认真分析，或可得窥英汉句式差异之一斑。

四、常见的翻译方法

1. 直译法与意译法

直译是指使译文基本上保持原文的形式和内容，同时要做到译文通顺，表达清楚。直译强调的是“形似”，力求在译文中保留原文的词序、语气、文体，甚至修辞手法等。意译与直译相反，指的是将原文的内容用释义的形式以译语表达出来。意译重在“神似”，所以不拘泥于原文的词序、语序、语气、文体等语言形式，也不拘泥于原文的各种句法结构及其功能。

(1) 直译法

直译法适用于译文和原文相通时。

例 12：

The proof of the pudding is in the eating.

要知道布丁的滋味，就要亲自尝一尝。

例 13：

清明是中国的二十四节气之一。

Qingming is one of the twenty-four Chinese solar terms.

（2）意译法

意译法适用于原文与译文不对等时。

例 14：

One boy is a boy, two boys half a boy, three boys no boy.

一个和尚挑水喝，两个和尚抬水喝，三个和尚没水喝。

例 15：

中国的传统节日形式多样，内容丰富，是我们民族悠久历史文化的一个重要组成部分。

Chinese traditional festivals, various in forms and rich in content, are is an important component of the long history and culture of Chinese people.

直译和意译是表达问题的方式。在翻译的过程当中，哪种方式更能较好地体现“忠实和通顺”抑或是“信和达”的翻译标准，就采取哪种方式。能直译时则直接翻译，不能直译则意译；需要直译和意译相结合时，那就在直译的基础上意译，或曰直译和意译参半。正如茅盾先生所说：“直译的意义若就浅处说，只是‘不妄改原文的字句’；就深处说，还求‘能保留原文的情调与风格’。”

2. 分句法与合句法

分句法是指把一个句子分拆成多个句子或者多个小句的翻译方法。分句法与合句法一样，都是对原文的句子结构做出调整，使之符合译文的表达规律。一般而言，因为英语句子较长且结构较复杂，翻译成汉语时更多地使用分句法；而汉语的句子较短且散，翻译成英语时更多地使用合句法。但这不是死板的规定。英译汉也可能会使用合句法，而汉译英也可能会使用分句法。

（1）长句的分译

例 16：

It was sufficient that there was tenderness in her eyes, weakness in her manner, good nature and hope in her thoughts.

译文：只要她眼睛里含情脉脉，举止里透露着娇柔，思想里洋溢着善良和希望，这就够了。

例 17：

The good tidings filled the whole nation with joy.

译文：捷报传来，举国欢腾。

例 18：

It is of great importance that we should keep in mind what we're strive for.

译文：我们应把奋斗的目标牢记在心，这一点极其重要。

（2）分句合译

例 19：

要是能像那种人一样，那该多有面子啊。

译文：It'd be magnificent to be like that person.

例 20：

有一点是不容置疑的，他们达成协议的意愿很强烈。

译文：No doubt that their intention to reach an agreement is strong.

例 21：

不要害怕那些思想可能会比你优秀的人，也不要害怕那些甚至比你更聪明的人。

译文：Don't be afraid of those who might have a better idea or who might even be more intelligent than you are.

例 22：

His eyes were triumphantly cold. There was no light in them, no feeling, no interest.

译文：他的目光傲慢冷酷、呆滞无光、淡漠无情。

例 23：

They don't look happy. They look angry, frightened or depressed.

译文：看样子他们不是高兴，而是生气、害怕，或者沮丧。

3. 增译法与减译法

汉英两种语言在词汇和句式方面存在诸多差异，导致在翻译时，为了使译文准确通顺，增减一些在结构上或表意上必需的词就十分必要。增译法即增词翻译，减译法即从略翻译。

这种增减或可体现在单个词的翻译上，如 modernization 译为现代化，efficient 译为高效（less efficient 译为低效），customer loyalty 译为客户忠诚度，importance 译为重要性，close 译为关上，silently 译为悄悄地，your 译为你的等。

（1）增译法

例 24：

Histories make men wise; poets witty; the mathematics subtle; natural philosophy deep; moral grave; logic and rhetoric able to contend.

译文：读史使人明智，读诗使人灵秀，数学使人周密，科学使人深刻，伦理使人庄重，逻辑修辞之学使人善辩。

例 25：

Modern life give people a dilemma: money, or health?

译文：现代生活方式使人左右两难：要钱，还是要健康？

例 26：

班门弄斧。

译文：Showing off one's proficiency with the axe before Lu Ban, the master carpenter.

例 27：

材料方面有了突破，产品质量就能提升。

译文：Product quality will improve when material breakthrough is achieved.

（2）减译法

例 28：

The earth goes around the sun.

译文：地球绕太阳转。

例 29：

A wise man will not marry a woman who has attainments but no virtue.

译文：聪明的人是不会娶有才无德的女子为妻的。

例 30：

The harmful side effect of this new drug is still unknown.

译文：这种新药的副作用尚不可知。

例 31：

The higher you stand, the more you can see.

译文：站得越高，看到的越多。

例 32：

粗糙的表面会增大摩擦力。

译文：The rush surface will increase friction.

4. 转换法

通常转换法主要是指词类的转换和句子的转换，后者又分为句子结构的转换和句子属性的转换。

（1）词类转换

由于英汉两种语言中词类的区别（如前所述），在翻译时，转换词类是保证译文通顺的必要之举。词类转换法也是翻译中最灵活多变的。

例 33：

The full moon is high up in the night sky.

译文：圆月高挂夜空。（形容词—动词）

例 34：

People believe what they see over what they hear.

译文：人们相信眼见胜过耳闻。（介词—动词）

例 35：

Action speaks louder than words.

译文：行动胜于雄辩。（名词—动词）

例 36：

The game was over.

译文：游戏结束了。（副词—动词）

例 37：

The hospitality of the hosting country impressed me deeply.

译文：主办国的热情给了我深刻的印象。（动词—名词，副词—形容词）

例 38：

鉴于会议十分重要，各方均按时赶到了会场。

译文：All parties involved went to the conference on time, since it was of great importance.（形容词—名词）

例 39：

作为一名决策者，他专业合格，心理却不过关。

译文：As a decision-maker, he is professionally qualified yet mentally not.（名词—副词）

例 40：

幸运的是，他找到了丢失的钥匙。

译文：Luckily, he found the lost key.（形容词—副词）

（2）句子转换

在翻译过程中，除了词类需要转换之外，句子也可以转换。需注意的是，无论是词类转换还是句子转换，都是为了使译文能更准确通顺地传达原文的意思。句子层次的转译，既可以是句子的语法属性发生变化，也可以是句子结构发生变化。

例 41：

As is known to all, the speed of light is higher than that of sound.

译文：众所周知，光速大于声速。（被动语态—主动语态）

例 42：

Vegetables should be watered regularly so that they can grow prosperously.

译文：蔬菜要生长得茂盛，就得定时灌溉。（目的从句—条件从句）

例 43：

My grandparents believed that you were either honest or dishonest.

译文：我爷爷奶奶认为人要么诚实，要么就不诚实。（分拆句子，重复用词）

例 44：

Despite the nasty weather, he went to work everyday.

译文：他天天去上班，尽管天气恶劣。（名词短语—主谓句）

例 45：

Though poor, mother bought me a series of books every month.

译文：母亲虽然穷，但还是每月给我买一系列的书籍。（省略—补充完整）

例 46：

昨晚下了大雨，把路都淹了，我就在办公室待了一晚。

译文：Yesterday the heavy rain flooded the road, so I stayed in the office for the night.（主谓句—名词短语，无主句—主谓句）

5. 重复法

如果原文中有出于修辞目的和语法需要而重复用词的地方，译文也依照原文的措辞方式进行表达，这不是翻译中的重复法。相反，翻译中的重复法，一般是指在原文中没有重复用词，而是译者根据语言差异和译文表达的需要，选择重复用词进行翻译的方法。

例 47：

他在凄雨中荡来荡去，想了又想，盘算了又盘算。

译文：He wandered about in the chill rain, thinking and thinking, brooding and brooding.

在例 47 的译文中，最直观的翻译方法是直译法，而非重复法。参看下面的重复翻译法例句：

例 48：

We have to analyze and solve problems.

译文：我们要分析问题，解决问题。

例 49：

The president, together with his managers, has agreed to develop new market in this region.

译文：对于在该地区开拓新市场，经理们都认可，董事长也认可。

例 50：

In that interview, he mentioned his parents who raised him as well as his friends who helped him.

译文：在采访中，他不但谈到了帮助过他的朋友们，而且还谈到了养育了他的父母。

6. 正译法和反译法

正译法即反说正译，而反译法则是正说反译。具体操作时并无严格要求，而是以准确通顺的表达为依据。英汉在措辞和表达上有诸多差异，如单词 good，可以正译为“好”，也可以反译为“不错”；而句子 Tom knows English. 既可以正译为“汤姆会英语”，也可以反译为“汤姆不会别的（语言）”。正反译法属于修辞范畴，其目的在于，在特定的语言环境下，使译文能够更恰当地表达原文的意思。

例 51：

甜而不腻。

译文：Agreeable sweetness.

例 52：

He shot at a bird but missed it.

译文：他向一只鸟射击但没打中。

例 53：

What he said is beyond our understanding.

译文：我们理解不了他的话。

例 54：

His ignorance in history resulted in his failure in the interview.

译文：由于对历史一无所知，他未能通过面试。

例 55：

I can't agree with you more.

译文：我极其赞同你的意见。

例 56：

If you need any help, please don't hesitate to tell me.

译文：如果需要帮助，请尽管说。

例 57：

油漆未干。

译文：Wet paint.

第二章 中国传统艺术
Chinese Traditional Arts

第一部分 简介

众所周知，中国传统艺术有着辉煌而悠久的历史，其遗产极其丰富，其中最具代表性的有书法、绘画、音乐、戏曲、雕刻、传统服饰等。它们在中国五千多年的文化长河中犹如一颗颗璀璨的明珠。中国传统艺术不仅体现了中国人民自身对美的追求，更是中华民族乃至全人类的宝贵财富。中国传统艺术以其浓郁的乡土气息、淳厚的艺术内涵和生动的历史痕迹，越来越受到世界人民的喜爱和推崇，成为人类共同的文化“大餐”。

It is common knowledge that China has a long and glorious history in its arts. Of all the abundant Chinese art heritages, the most representatives are calligraphy, painting, music, opera, sculpture and traditional clothes etc., which are brilliant pearls in Chinese culture for over five thousand years. They are not only the embodiment of the people's longing for aesthetic beauty for themselves but also great treasures for China and the rest of the world. Chinese traditional arts are increasingly favored and appreciated by more and more people because of their full-bodied local flavors, rich artistic connotations and vivid historical traces. They are enjoyed as a cultural feast by all the people in the world.

第二部分 词汇

Chinese expressions	English expressions
1. 京剧	Beijing Opera
2. 国粹	quintessence
3. 唱、念、做、打	singing, dialogue, dancing and acrobatic fighting
4. 生、旦、净、丑	Sheng (male), Dan (female), Jing (painted face), Chou (clown)
5. 传播、宣传	propagate
6. 川剧	Sichuan Opera
7. 变脸	face changing
8. 粤剧	Cantonese Opera
9. 越剧	Shaoxing Opera
10. 皮影戏	shadow play
11. 皮影	shadow puppet
12. 人物剪影	articulated figure
13. 照明，照射	illuminate
14. 操纵	manipulate

续 表

Chinese expressions	English expressions
15. 精美的	exquisite
16. 雕刻	sculpture, engrave，carve
17. 书法	calligraphy
18. 汉字	Chinese character
19. 宣纸	rice paper
20. 书房	the study (n.)
21. 文房四宝	The Four Treasures of the Chinese Study
22. 笔墨纸砚	writing brush, ink, rice paper, and inkstone
23. 文化艺术修养	cultural and artistic accomplishment
24. 篆书	bronze inscriptions
25. 隶书	official script
26. 行书	regular script
27. 楷书	cursive script
28. 草书	running script
29. 国画	traditional Chinese painting
30. 颜料	colored pigment
31. 追溯到	trace back to, date back to
32. 新石器时代陶器	Neolithic pottery
33. 题材	genre
34. 体现	embody
35. 印章	seal
36. 人物画	figure painting
37. 山水画	landscape painting
38. 花鸟画	bird-and-flower painting
39. 审美情趣	aesthetic sentiment
40. 玉雕	jade carving
41. 牙雕	tooth carving
42. 木雕	wood carving

续　表

Chinese expressions	English expressions
43. 石雕	stone carving
44. 竹刻	bamboo carving
45. 骨刻	bone carving
46. 国家瑰宝	national gem
47. 中国传统服饰	Chinese traditional costumes
48. 衣冠王国	The Kingdom of Dress
49. 兼容并包	inclusive
50. 东方韵味	oriental charm
51. 文化载体	cultural carrier
52. 汉服	Han costumes (Hanfu)
53. 唐装	Tang costumes (Tangzhuang)
54. 旗袍	Cheongsam (Qipao)
55. 生命力，活力	vitality
56. 艺术感染力	artistic appeal
57. 马褂	Magua
58. 满族服饰	Manchu clothing
59. 西式立体剪裁	western solid cutting
60. 亚太经合组织	APEC
61. 唐人街	Chinatown
62. 流行起来	come into vogue/catch on
63. 端庄	civility
64. 东方特质	oriental idiosyncrasy
65. 装饰手法	ornamental technique
66. 民族风格	national flavor
67. 国际时装舞台	international fashion arena
68. 电影节	film festival
69. 世界小姐大赛	Miss World pageant contest
70. 世界模特大赛	global model contest

续 表

Chinese expressions	English expressions
71. 战国	Warring States
72. 中国古代文人	scholars of ancient China
73. 人类非物质文化遗产名录	Masterpieces of the Intangible Cultural Heritage of Humanity
74. 汉族	the Han nationality
75. 黄帝	Yellow Emperor
76. 千年	millennium

第三部分 文化精选

1. 京剧

京剧是中国最大的戏曲剧种，有“国剧”之称，是地道的国粹，被誉为“东方歌剧”。它起源于中国多种古老的地方戏剧，特别是南方的“徽班”。到了 19 世纪末，京剧吸收了其他地方剧种、艺术门类之所长，形成了独特的艺术风格和相当完整的表演体系，成为中国戏剧文化的代表。京剧是一门集唱音乐、表演、文学、歌唱、化妆和服装为一体的舞台艺术，通过唱、念、做、打四大艺术形式来呈现戏剧、刻画人物。京剧中的角色主要有生（男性）、旦（女性）、净（男性）、丑（男性、女性皆有）四大行当。京剧走遍世界各地，成为介绍、传播中国传统文化的重要手段。

1.Beijing Opera

Beijing Opera, the largest Chinese opera, is regarded as the national opera of China. Originated from many kinds of ancient local operas, especially from Huiban in southern China，Beijing Opera has become the genuine national quintessence and is extolled as Oriental Opera. At the end of the 19th Century, a whole complete set of artistic style and performing system of Beijing Opera took shape from absorbing many other local dramatic forms and art categories. Since then Beijing Opera has become the representative of China dramas. It is a scenic art integrating music, performance, literature, singing, makeup and costume. Beijing Opera presents dramatic plays and figures mainly by infusing four artistic methods: singing, dialogue, dancing and fighting. The main types of roles in it are Sheng (male), Dan (female), Jing (painted face), Chou (clown). Beijing Opera is spread all over the world and has become the important means to introduce and propagate the Chinese traditional culture.

2. 变脸

川剧起源于明末清初。“变脸”是川剧的亮点，是一种瞬间多次变换脸部妆容的表演艺术，用于揭示剧中人物的不同思想与感情。相传“变脸”是古人在面对凶猛野兽时为了生存，把自己脸部用不同的方式勾画出不同的形态，以此来吓跑入侵的猛兽。川剧把“变脸”搬上舞台，用绝妙的技巧使它成为一门独特的艺术。变脸是一种神奇的艺术，表演者能在20秒内变换十张脸。通过抬手、舞袖、摆头的动作，演员变换不同的脸谱来表达惊恐、绝望、愤怒等不同的情感，用有形的面具来揭示无形的内心世界。

2.Face Changing

Sichuan Opera (Chuan Ju) originated at the end of the Ming Dynasty and the beginning of the Qing Dynasty. Face changing is the highlight of Sichuan Opera. It refers to the special performance skill of changing facial masks several times in the blink of an eye to show different emotions and feelings of the characters in the play. Allegedly, the talent was used to scare away fierce beasts. In order to survive, people painted their faces with different patterns to threaten wild animals. Sichuan Opera performers present the skill on stage and have made it a unique art. Face changing is a magical art. How wonderful it is for actors to change more than 10 masks in less than 20 seconds! By raising the hand, swinging a sleeve or tossing the head, an actor uses different masks to show different emotions such as panic, despair and anger, expressing invisible and intangible feelings through visible and tangible masks.

3. 皮影戏

中国皮影艺术，是我国民间工艺与戏曲巧妙结合而成的独特艺术形式，是中华民族艺术殿堂里不可或缺的一颗璀璨的明珠。皮影戏是一种用灯光照射兽皮或纸板做成的人物剪影以表演故事的民间戏剧形式。表演时，艺人在音乐的伴奏下，一边操纵剪影一边演唱。中国皮影戏历史悠久，相传起源于汉朝，兴盛于唐朝和宋朝，是中国出现最早的戏曲剧种之一。皮影艺术堪称当今影视艺术的鼻祖。皮影戏因其余音绕梁的音乐、精美的雕刻、明快的颜色和生动的表演赢得了观众的喜爱。而绚丽的色彩、优雅的造型、流畅的线条，让皮影不仅仅是道具，更是艺术品。

3.Shadow Play

Chinese shadow puppet art, a special form of art skillfully combining folk arts crafts with drama in China, is an indispensable exquisite pearl in the palace of Chinese folk arts. Shadow puppet play is a folk opera form of cutting beast skin or hard paper board into articulated figures and performing in front of an illuminated backdrop to create the illusion of moving images. Accompanied by music, performers manipulate the figures by pulling the strings and sing. With a long history, shadow puppet play is said to stem from the Han Dynasty and flourish in the Tang and Song Dynasties. It is one of the earliest Chinese opera form. Shadow puppet art is considered to be the ancestor of today's film and television art. Shadow play wins the heart of audience by its lingering music, exquisite sculpture, brisk color and lively performance. The flowery color, elegant sculpting and smooth lines make shadow puppets not only a piece of props but also an artwork.

4. 书法

书法是中国传统文化中特有的文化，被认为是中国文化中最抽象和卓越的艺术形式，在中国传统艺术中占据着显著的地位。中国书法是一门汉字书写艺术，以“文房四宝”——笔、墨、纸、砚为工具。书写者使用毛笔，蘸取适量的墨汁，在宣纸上书写。书法不仅是表达观念的符号，更是表情达意的形态。“字如其人”，因此书法可以体现一个人的文化和艺术修养。好的书法是书写人的情感和书法技巧与宣纸、毛笔、中国墨的完美结合。书法经历了2 000多年的发展，演变成为五大具有不同技巧的书写体式：篆书、隶书、行书、楷书、草书。

4.Chinese Calligraphy

As a unique traditional culture, Chinese calligraphy is regarded as the most abstract and sublime form of art in Chinese culture and occupies a distinguished position in the field of traditional art. Chinese calligraphy is a writing art of Chinese characters. To practice calligraphy requires the basic tools of the Four Treasures of the Study including writing brush, ink, rice paper, and inkstone as well as much concentration on guiding the soft writing brush charged with fluid ink, and writing on rice paper. Chinese calligraphy is not only a symbol of showing one's opinions, but also a means of expressing his inner world. As the saying goes "The style of one's character represents the man", people can read the handwriter's culture and art cultivation from his works. Fine calligraphy is a perfect integration of hand-writer's emotion, excellent handwriting technique, rice paper, brush and Chinese ink. Calligraphy has endured for more than 2,000 years, and evolved into five main ways of writing each with different techniques: bronze inscriptions, official script, regular script, cursive script and running script.

5. 国画

国画是中国文化遗产的重要组成部分，它是用毛笔、墨和中国画颜料在特制的宣纸或绢上作画。国画历史悠久，其根源可以追溯到约 6 000 年前新石器时代陶器上的绘画。题材主要分为人物、山水和花鸟三类。和西方绘画不同，中国画以其神韵和意境著称。国画是一种融合诗歌、书法、绘画和印章为一体的艺术形式，在思想内容和艺术创作上，反映了中华民族的精神面貌和审美情趣，体现了中国人对自然、社会、人生等方面的认识。其艺术成就和民族特色赢得了世界人民的认可，日益为世界现代艺术借鉴与吸收。

5.Traditional Chinese Painting

As an important part of the country's cultural heritage, traditional Chinese painting is an art of painting on a piece of rice paper or silk with a Chinese brush that was soaked with black ink or colored pigments. Its roots can be traced back to paintings on Neolithic pottery some 6,000 years ago. It developed and was classified by theme into three genres: figures, landscapes, and birds-and-flowers. Different from Western painting, Chinese painting is distinguished by a spirit and an atmosphere all its own. It is a blend of poetry, calligraphy, painting and seal carving. Its contents and artistic creation reflect the national spirit and the Chinese aesthetic sentiment and embody the people's understanding of nature, society, and life,etc.Its artistic achievement and national features have won recognition of the people all over the world, which are being increasingly used for reference by modern artists.

6. 雕刻

中国雕刻艺术技艺精湛，品类繁多，是人类文化艺术宝库中一颗璀璨的明珠。其历史悠久，经过漫长的发展进程保存并得以发展。因为其显著的文化差异，中西方雕刻艺术迥然不同。人物、动物、植物或景观都可以被艺术家精致地雕刻。中国艺术家可以在一系列的原材料如石、牙、角、根和竹子上展示他们的才华和创造力。中国雕刻艺术中最为出名的几种有玉雕、牙雕、木雕、石雕、竹刻、骨刻等。

6.Chinese Carving Art

With exquisite skill and rich variety, Chinese carving art is a lustrous pearl in the treasure-house of culture and art of mankind. With a time-honored history, it has survived and thrived in its long developing process. Due to prominent cultural differences, Chinese carving art varies greatly from its counterpart in the West. Objects such as figures, animals, plants or landscapes are delicately carved by artists. Chinese artists demonstrate their talents and creativity on a range of raw materials from stone, tooth, horn, root, and bamboo,etc. therefore forming the schools of carving as jade carving, tooth carving, wood carving, stone carving, bamboo carving and bone carving.

7. 传统服饰

中国素有"衣冠王国"之称。几千年来，中华各民族创造了无数精美绝伦的服饰。服饰既是人们生活的必需品，也是文化载体，反映着特定历史时期的社会制度、经济生活、民俗风情，也承载着人们的思想文化和审美观念。兼容并包、异彩纷呈而又独具东方韵味的中国传统服饰向世界展示了中国文化和中国人的智慧。尽管时尚潮流随时间而变化，但直到今天仍有几种传统服饰在国内外深受欢迎，如汉服、唐装和旗袍。近年来，在一些颇具影响力的国际时装秀中，都不乏中国传统服饰的元素，这说明中国传统服饰具有强大的生命力和艺术感染力。

7.Chinese Traditional Costumes

China has always enjoyed the reputation of "the Kingdom of Dress". For thousands of years, the Chinese created numerous exquisite costumes. As an essential part of human life, clothing is also a kind of cultural carrier. It reflects the social system, economic life and folk customs at the specific historical period and carries the people's cultural and aesthetic ideas. The combination of Chinese clothing with its inclusivity, splendor, and unique oriental charms shows the world the Chinese culture and the Chinese wisdom. Although the fashion trend has always been changing, several types of Chinese traditional costumes are still popular both at home and abroad such as Han(Hanfu),Tang costumes(Tangzhuang) and Cheongsam(Qipao). In recent years, the elements of the traditional Chinese dress highlight and catch people's eyes in some influential international fashion shows. Chinese traditional clothing has always caught on with its strong vitality and artistic appeal.

8. 唐装

唐装是中式服装的通称，是传统和现代的结合品。现在的唐装源自清朝满族的一种服饰——马褂，将中国传统元素和西式立体剪裁结合在了一起。“唐装”这个词最初来源于海外华人。因为唐朝的盛誉，中国人被外国人称为“唐人”，海外华人居住的地方因而被称为“唐人街”，他们的服装被称为“唐装”。2001 年亚太经合组织会议各国元首身着唐装集体亮相，唐装由此而出名。自此，这种新型的服装被公认为唐装，在海内外深受欢迎。

8.Tang Costumes (Tangzhuang)

Tang costume (Tangzhuang), a general term for Chinese costumes, is the integrity of traditional costumes and modern ones. The modern one evolves from the Magua of the Qing Dynasty which is a kind of Manchu clothing, a style of minority in north China. It combines traditional Chinese elements and western dyapiag or cauge cutting style. The word "Tangzhuang" itself was originally created by overseas Chinese. Because of the high reputation of the Tang Dynasty, Chinese people are called "Tang People" by foreigners; thus the place where overseas Chinese reside in has been called "Chinatown",and their costume is called "Tangzhuang". It became famous in 2001 when heads of different countries appeared in APEC wearing Tangzhuang. From then on, this new kind of clothing has been regarded as Chinese Tangzhuang and has enjoyed tremendous popularity both at home and abroad.

9. 旗袍

旗袍是中国最典型、最传统的女性服饰之一，被誉为中国传统服饰文化的典范。它源自清代满族女性服饰。到了 20 世纪 20 年代，受西方服饰的影响，经过改良后的旗袍逐渐在广大妇女中流行起来，在 20 世纪 30 年代，几乎成为中国妇女的标准服装。旗袍——根据东方女性的体型进行剪裁并配上浓厚的东方特质的装饰，将东方女性的端庄、典雅、娇媚和性感展露无遗。旗袍以浓郁的民族风格体现了中华民族传统的服饰美。在中国漫长的服装文化历史中，旗袍跨越了国界，走上国际时装舞台，成为代表中国传统文化的时尚服装，并受到了很多外国女性的喜爱。如今，不论是各大电影节还是世界小姐、世界模特大赛上，旗袍已经成为一种中国服饰的代名词。

9.Cheongsam(Qipao)

Cheongsam is one of the most typical, traditional costumes for Chinese women and has been viewed as the model of Chinese traditional clothing culture. It has its origin in the Manchu female's costumes in the Qing Dynasty. In the 1920s, influenced by Western dress, cheongsam gradually came into vogue after improved, and was nearly became the standard garment for women in the 1930s. Cheongsam, properly and well cut by the oriental female body shape with adorning unique oriental characteristics, well demonstrates the modesty, the elegance, and the charm of the oriental females. Cheongsam features strong national flavor and embodies the beauty of Chinese traditional costumes. Throughout the long history of Chinese clothing culture, cheongsam has gone beyond national borders and entered the international fashion arena. It has become the fashion style representing Chinese traditional culture and has become popular with many foreign ladies. Today, cheongsam has become synonymous with Chinese fashion, whether it is at film festivals, Miss World pageants or global model contests.

第四部分 翻译练习

把下面短文翻译成英语或汉语：

10. 印章

印章就是图章，它在中国文化中的角色不容小觑，无论是公事还是私事都要用到印章。据史料记载，印章在战国时期已普遍使用。印章手工雕刻而成，形状以圆、方为主。印章雕刻是结合了书法和雕刻之美的一种古代艺术。印章除应用于日常事务之外，还常用于书画题识，逐渐成为中国特有的艺术形式之一。

11. 文房四宝

只要提到中国文化，就能想到文房四宝。文房四宝是中国独具特色的文书工具，是中国文化不可缺少的部分。笔墨纸砚是中国古代文人书房中必备的宝贝，故被称为“文房四宝”。用笔墨书写和绘画的历史在中国可追溯到五千年前。正是文房四宝推动着中国的书法和绘画的发展，可以说文房四宝书写着整个中华文明。

12. Cantonese Opera

Cantonese Opera, a traditional opera of our country, is praised as a red bean in South China by Premier Zhou Enlai. It is prevalent in Gunagdong, Guangxi, Hong Kong and Macao. Cantonese Opera is composed of drama and art in different places of China. It is one of the largest drama classes in Guangdong. Cantonese Opera started at the end of the Ming Dynasty and has a history of over three hundred years. During this period, it has undergone ups and downs that have made a great change to Cantonese Opera. Today it has become a blend of conventional Cantonese folk melodies, popular songs, modern Cantonese instrumental compositions and even Western tunes. Cantonese opera has been enlisted into Masterpieces of the Intangible Cultural Heritage of Humanity.

13. Han Costumes

Han costume, the traditional dress of Han Chinese people, is representative of the characteristics of the Han nationality. It became known as “Hanfu” because the fashion was popularized during the Han Dynasty. Hanfu reflects the rituals of Chinese culture from that era. Hanfu has a history of more than three millennia, and is said to have been worn by the legendary Yellow Emperor. This kind of garments was representative of ancient Oriental Civilization spanning millenniums.

第五部分 练习参考译文

10. Seal

A seal can also be defined as a stamp. The role of seals in the Chinese culture can hardly be underestimated. They have been used in both official and private spheres. According to the historical records, seals were widely used during the Warring States Period. Seals are engraved by hand basically shaped as round or square. Seal engraving is an art form that combines the essence of both calligraphy and carving. Chinese seals are not only used in daily life, but also used to represent signatures on paintings and calligraphies. It is gradually becoming one of China's unique artworks.

11. The Four Treasures of the Study

When it comes to Chinese culture, the Four Treasures of the Study, which are the unique writing tools in China, fall on people's minds. They are an essential part of the Chinese culture. The writing brush, ink, rice paper, and inkstone were requisite treasures in the study of the scholars of ancient China; hence they are often referred to as "the Four Treasures of the Study". The writing brush and ink stick have been used by the Chinese to write and paint since 5,000 years ago. It is the Four Treasures of the Study that have been driving the development of Chinese calligraphy and painting. Indeed, the Four Treasures of the Study have written the whole Chinese civilization.

12. 粤剧

粤剧是我国传统的戏剧，曾被周恩来总理誉为“南国红豆”，盛行于广东、广西、香港、澳门等地。粤剧集合了中国不同地方的戏曲艺术，为广东最大的戏曲剧种之一。粤剧始于明末，至今已有三百多年的历史，期间经历过的起伏使粤剧有了重大的变化。

今天的粤剧融传统的广东民间音乐、流行歌曲、现代器乐演奏甚至西方音乐为一体。粤剧已被列入人类非物质文化遗产名录。

13. 汉服

汉服是中国汉族人的传统服饰，反映着汉民族的特征，因为流行于汉朝而被称为“汉服”。它反映了当时的文化习俗。汉服有着 3 000 多年的历史，据说最早为传说中的黄帝所穿。这种服饰是中国几千年古老东方文明的代表。

第三章　中国民间工艺
Chinese Folk Arts & Crafts

第一部分 简介

中国传统民间手工艺品是指民间人们为适应生活需要和审美要求，就地取材，以手工生产为主的一种工艺美术品。手工艺品的品种非常繁多，如宋锦、竹编、草编、手工刺绣、蓝印花布、蜡染、手工木雕、泥塑、剪纸、民间玩具等。由于各地区、各民族的社会历史、风俗习尚、地理环境、审美观点的不同，各地的手工艺品具有不同的风格特色，充分展示了中国手工艺术的风采。手工制作工艺以其悠久的历史、精湛的技艺、丰富的门类、传世佳作蜚声海内外，是中华民族文化艺术的瑰宝。几千年来，传统手工艺始终是代表中华民族的一大特色产业。

Chinese traditional folk arts and crafts refer to the artistic handicrafts made with local materials by common people for the purposes of living and aesthetic appreciation. There are a wide variety of handicrafts such as brocade of Song Dynasty, bamboo weaving, straw plaited article, embroidery, blue cloth with design in white, batik, wood carving, clay sculpture, paper-cutting and folk toys, etc. They fully manifest the beauty of Chinese arts with their different features and styles, which come from the diverse social histories, customs and practices, geographical environment and aesthetic standards. Folk arts and crafts, the precious gems of Chinese arts, enjoy a high reputation both at home and abroad for their long history, fine craftsmanship, wide variety products and classics. For thousands of years, traditional handicrafts are always the representative characteristic industry of China.

第二部分 词汇

Chinese expressions	English expressions
1. 剪纸	paper-cutting
2. 传统手工艺品	traditional handicraft
3. 富有民族特色	with distinctive ethnic features
4. 民间工艺	folk art
5. 立春	the beginning of spring

续　表

Chinese expressions	English expressions
6. 迎春	welcome spring
7. 镂空玲珑的效果	exquisite visual effect
8. 视觉艺术	visual art
9. 栩栩如生的	true to life
10. 胖娃娃抱鲤鱼	plump children cuddling carp
11. 喜鹊登枝	magpie on wintersweet
12. 天官赐福	heavenly god blesses the people
13. 五谷丰登	a golden harvest
14. 龙凤呈祥	prosperity brought by the loong and the phoenix
15. 非物质文化遗产	intangible cultural heritage
16. 四大名绣	the four most famous embroideries
17. 苏绣	Su Embroidery / Suzhou Embroidery
18. 湘绣	Xiang Embroidery / Hunan Embroidery
19. 蜀绣	Shu Embroidery / Sichuan Embroidery
20. 粤绣	Yue Embroidery / Guangdong Embroidery
21. 发绣	Hair Embroidery
22. 绣线	embroidery thread
23. 闺阁绣	boudoir embroidery
24. 宫廷绣	court embroidery / palace embroidery
25. 单面绣	single-side embroidery
26. 双面绣	double-side embroidery
27. 风格独特	unique style
28. 绸或绢	silk or tough silk
29. 顾绣	Gu Embroidery
30. 龙凤	loong and phoenix
31. 飞禽走兽	fowls and beasts
32. 增加喜庆的气氛	enhance the joyous atmosphere

续　表

Chinese expressions	English expressions
33. 百鸟朝凤	Hundreds of Birds Worshiping Phoenix
34. 八仙过海	the Eight Immortals Crossing the Sea
35. 农历	lunar calendar
36. 点灯笼	light lanterns
37. 灯火辉煌	brilliantly illuminated
38. 元宵节	Lantern Festival
39. 国家繁荣昌盛	the prosperous, strong and powerful country
40. 红灯笼	red lantern
41. 宫灯	palace lanterns
42. 里层	inner layer
43. 彩灯	colorful bulbs
44. 除夕	New Year's Eve/the eve of the Spring Festival
45. 灯展	lantern show/lantern fair
46. 灯谜	lantern riddles
47. 代表	stand for
48. 彩塑	painted sculpture
49. 原料	raw material
50. 春秋战国时期	the Spring and Autumn Period and the Warring States Period
51. 达到顶峰	reach the peak
52. 景泰蓝	cloisonné
53. 敦煌莫高窟	Mogao Caves / Mogao Grottoes at Dunhuang
54. 晋祠	Jin Memorial Temple
55. 流派	school
56. 泥人张	Clay Figurine Zhang
57. 青花瓷	blue-and-white porcelain
58. 瓷都	the capital of porcelain

续　表

Chinese expressions	English expressions
59. 官窑	the official kiln
60. 唐三彩	tri-colored glazed pottery of the Tang Dynasty
61. 粉彩瓷	famille-rose porcelain
62. 造纸业	paper-making industry
63. 吉祥的	auspicious
64. 中国结	Chinese knot
65. 放风筝	kite-flying
66. 栽桑树	mulberry planting
67. 开辟新纪元	opening up a new era
68. 东方文明	oriental civilization
69. 养蚕	sericulture
70. 缫丝	silk reeling

第三部分 文化精选

14. 剪纸

剪纸是深受人们喜爱的中国传统工艺。它是用剪刀将彩纸剪成各种装饰图案，故称为“剪纸”。剪纸起源于公元前 6 世纪的西周时期。在当时，女子有使用金银箔和彩帛剪成花鸟贴在鬓角为饰的风尚。中国最早的剪纸作品发现于北朝时期（386—581）。到了唐代（618—907），剪纸艺术开始大放光彩。后来，人们在婚嫁寿宴或节日期间将剪纸贴在墙上、窗上、门上、家具什物上以表达吉祥庆贺的意思，增加喜庆气氛。剪纸还可以用于祭祀祭天等郑重的仪式。

14.Paper-cutting

Paper-cutting is a wide popular folk art. People cut colorful paper with scissors to form various decorative patterns and that is where the name came from. Paper-cutting originated from the 6th century of the Xizhou Dynasty when women had the fashion to paste on their hair at the temples with golden and silver foil or colored silk cut into flower or bird figures. The earliest paper-cutting was found during the Northern Dynasties (A.D 386-581) and began to prevail in Tang Dynasty (A.D. 618-907). People paste paper-cutting works on walls, windows, doors and furniture at wedding ceremonies, birthday parties or festivals to bring auspicious blessings and enhance the festive atmosphere. They are also used in sacred rituals such as worshiping their ancestors and gods.

15. 刺绣

刺绣是中国传统工艺中的一朵奇葩。最早的刺绣可追溯到商朝（约前 1600—前 1046），在当时是身份地位的象征。随着经济的发展，刺绣才进入寻常百姓家。到了宋代，刺绣的质量和数量都达到了顶峰。如今，中国的刺绣工艺几乎遍布全国，苏州的苏绣、湖南的湘绣、四川的蜀绣、广东的粤绣各具特色，被誉为中国的四大名绣。发展到今天的刺绣艺术品，工艺精细复杂，成了非常唯美的工艺品，受到各国人民的赞赏和喜爱。

15.Embroidery

Embroidery is a brilliant pearl in Chinese traditional arts and crafts. The oldest embroidered product in China on record dates from the Shang Dynasty (about 1600-1046 B.C.). Embroidery in this period symbolized social status. It was not until later on, as the national economy developed, that embroidered products entered the lives of the common people. The Song Dynasty saw a peak of development of embroidery in both quantity and quality. Nowadays, embroidery is all over China. Suzhou embroidery, Hunan embroidery, Sichuan embroidery and Guangdong embroidery are the four most famous in China. The embroidered products of today are delicate and complicated and have become aesthetic handicrafts appreciated and enjoyed by the people all over the world.

16. 花灯

花灯，又名“彩灯”，是亚洲的一种传统民间工艺品，既有实用功能又有审美价值。灯笼源于东汉时期。在古代，其主要作用是照明，由纸或者绢作为灯笼的外皮，骨架通常使用竹或木条制作，中间放上蜡烛，点燃蜡烛成为照明工具。在亚洲的庙宇中，灯笼是相当常见的物品。如今，灯笼已经变成一种装饰品，佳节庆典中都要使用灯笼，特别是元宵节和中秋节。

16.Festive Lantern

Festive lantern, which is also named coloured lantern, is a

traditional folk craft in Asia. It is the combination of practical and aesthetic values. Originating from the Eastern Han Dynasty, lanterns mainly were used as lamps in ancient China. While paper and silk were the major outer materials of a lantern, bamboo and fine wood were used to make frames and a candle was placed inside to make it a lamp. Lanterns are usually seen in Asian temples. Nowadays they have become merely decorations and are used in grand ceremonies especially the Lantern Festival and Mid-Autumn Festival.

17. 泥塑

泥塑，俗称“彩塑”“泥玩”，是以泥土为原料，以手工捏制成各种形象的一种民间手工艺品。或素或彩，以人物、动物为主。中国泥塑艺术可上溯到距今两千多年前的春秋战国时期。到了唐宋时代，泥塑艺术达到了顶峰。著名泥塑有甘肃敦煌莫高窟的菩萨、山西太原晋祠的宫女等。至清代，泥塑最出名的是天津的“泥人张”和无锡的惠山泥人。中国非常重视非物质文化遗产的保护，2006 年 5 月 20 日，泥塑经国务院批准列入第一批国家级非物质文化遗产名录。

17.Clay Sculpture

Clay sculpture, also known as “painted sculpture” and “mud play”, is a kind of folk craft of sculpturing a wide variety of figures from clay by hand. They are plain in color or multi-colored and mainly take the shape of human figures and animals. Chinese clay sculpture art can be traced back to the Spring and Autumn Period and the Warring States Period. In the Tang and Song Dynasties, clay sculptures were at their peak. The famous sculptures were Bodhisattva of Mogao Grottoes at Dunhuang in Gansu province and the palace maid of Jin Memorial Temple in Taiyuan City, Shanxi Province. During the Qing Dynasty, there appeared two kinds of clay figurines which enjoyed the highest reputation across the country. One was from a master whose name was Clay Figurine Zhang in Tianjin and the other, the Huishan clay figurines made in Wuxi, Jiangsu Province. China attaches great importance to the protection of intangible cultural heritage. On May 20th, 2006, upon the approval of the State Council, clay sculpture was listed in the first batch of national intangible cultural heritage.

18. 瓷器

中国是瓷器的故乡，号称“瓷器之国”。瓷器的发明是中华民族对世界文明的伟大贡献。大约在公元前 16 世纪的商代，中国就出现了早期的瓷器。唐代是瓷器发展的顶峰，出现了著名的“唐三彩”。至宋代，江西的景德镇成为瓷业的中心。五代十国的时候出现了青花瓷，其釉色温润如玉，造型简洁秀美、自成一格。瓷器作为伟大的中国文化的象征，受到全世界人民的仰慕与赞叹。

18.Porcelain

China is the hometown of porcelain, and is renowned as

"the nation of porcelain". The invention of porcelain is of great contribution to the world civilization. It is believed that primitive porcelain ware emerged in Shang Dynasty in the 16th century B.C. The development of the art of porcelain reached its peak in the Tang Dynasty, as evidenced by the renowned "tri-colored glaze". Jingde Town became a principal centre of the porcelain industry during the Song Dynasty. Blue-and-white porcelain, a famous type of ancient Chinese stoneware, came into being during the period of the Five Dynasties and Ten Kingdoms. It is characterized by simple but refined shapes, jade-like glaze and a distinctive style. Chinese porcelain, as a symbol of the great Chinese culture, is admired and appreciated by the people all over the world.

19. 丝绸

中国是丝绸的故乡。栽桑、养蚕、缫丝、织绸是中国古代人民的伟大发明。商周时期丝绸的生产技术就已发展到相当高的水平。西汉时张骞出使西域，把中原与波斯湾、地中海紧密联系起来，开辟了中外交流贸易的新纪元。从此中国的丝绸以其卓越的品质、精美的花色和丰富的文化内涵闻名于世，成为中国文化的象征、东方文明的使者。

19.Chinese Silk

China is the home of silk. Mulberry planting, sericulture, silk reeling and thickening are all great inventions of the ancient Chinese.

As early as the Shang and Zhou Dynasties, the Chinese people's silk-weaving techniques had reached an extremely high level. During the Western Han Dynasty, Zhang Qian, an outstanding diplomat, travelled around central Asia and connected China with the Persian Gulf and the Mediterranean, opening up a new era of Sino-foreign trade, exchange and communication. From then on, China's silk became well known for its extraordinary quality, exquisite design and color, and abundant culture connotations. So far, Chinese silk has been accepted as a symbol of Chinese culture and an emissary of oriental civilization.

20. 中国结

中国结，是一种装饰手工艺品，是一种中国民间艺术形式。古称络子，历史悠久，并影响到周边国家的装饰艺术如日本结、朝鲜结。中国结不仅造型优美、色彩多样，同时作品的命名，如“吉庆有余”“福寿双全”“双喜临门”“吉祥如意”“一路顺风”等组配，都表示热烈浓郁的美好祝福，是赞颂以及传达衷心至诚的祈求和心愿的佳作。中国结从头到尾都是用一根丝线编结而成，每一个基本结又根据其形、意命名。把不同的结饰互相结合在一起，或用其他具有吉祥图案的饰物搭配组合，就形成了造型独特、绚丽多彩、寓意深刻、内涵丰富的中国传统吉祥装饰物品。

20.Chinese Knot

Chinese knot, a hand-made craft for decoration, is a folk art of China with a long history. Called “luozi” in the ancient times,

Chinese knots have influenced the decoration arts of nearby countries such as Japan and Korea. They are perfect artworks to express the traditional pleasant praises, warmest regards, best wishes and finest ideals with their refined shapes and various colours, in addition to the names such as "Full of Joy", "Happiness& Longevity", "Double Happiness", "Luck and Auspiciousness As One Wishes" and "Wish You a Fair Wind Journey". The characteristic of Chinese knots is that every knot is made of a single silk rope and named by its specific form and meaning. By combining different knots or other auspicious adornments skillfully, it becomes a traditional auspicious ornament full of meanings with its unique design and colors.

21. 风筝

风筝为中国人发明，是用细竹条做骨架，贴上鲜艳的纸或丝绸，再画上画。相传墨翟以木头制成木鸟，研制三年有成，是人类最早的风筝起源，后来其学生鲁班用竹子，改进墨翟的风筝材质，更进而演进成为今日的多线风筝。最早的风筝并不是玩具，而是用于军事、通信上。到南北朝，风筝开始成为传递信息的工具。从隋唐开始，由于造纸业的发达，民间开始用纸来裱糊风筝。唐代晚期，因为有人在风筝上加入了琴弦，风一吹，就发出像古筝那样的声音，于是就有了“风筝”的叫法。现在，放风筝已经成为人们喜爱的户外活动。

21.Kite

Kite was invented by ancient Chinese. It is made with slim bamboo as its frame and is covered with colorful painted paper or silk. As the story goes, Mo Zi, the prominent ideologist and statesman of the Warring States period, spent three years constructing a wooden bird, which was the origin of the kite in human history. Later his pupil, the master carpenter Lu Ban, improved the material, using the bamboo to make kite and it evolved into the strings kite of today. The earliest kites were used in military and telecommunication instead of entertainment. In the Southern and Northern Dynasties, kite became an instrument to send messages and from the Sui and Tang Dynasties, people began to use paper to cover the kite due to the prosperous paper-making industry. In the late Tang Dynasty, people added strings into the kite. It sounded like ancient zither when winds blew into it, and that was how it got the name "kite". Now kite-flying is a popular outdoor activity.

第四部分 翻译练习

把下面短文翻译成英语或汉语：

22. 西湖绸伞

西湖绸伞，以竹作骨，以绸张面，轻巧悦目，式样美观，携带方便，素有“西湖之花”的美称。它的伞面采用杭州丝绸，故名西湖绸伞。伞，在我国历史非常悠久，据说 4 000 多年前的黄帝时代就已制作。特别是明清时代，我国制伞业尤为发达，从那时起，不少小说和戏曲都有提到伞。众所周知，《白蛇传》中许仙借伞的故事，就发生在杭州西湖断桥边，这为西湖绸伞更增添了几分神话色彩。西湖绸伞既可遮挡烈日，又可作为精美的装饰品，集实用性与艺术性于一体，已成为我国独有的手工艺品之一。

23. 中国年画

中国民间年画，又称“门神”“喜画”，是中国欢庆春节时特有的一种书画刻印艺术。每值岁末，人们在大门口贴年画、对联，以祝愿新年吉庆、驱凶迎祥，增添节日的吉祥喜庆气氛。年画是中国民间最普及的艺术品之一。年画因一年一更换，或张贴后可供一年欣赏之用，故称“年画”。中国年画历史源远流长，表达了民众的思想感情和审美情趣以及向往美好生活的愿望。

24. Printing and Dyeing

Dyeing textiles using minerals and plants is a time-honored practice in China. Early in the Neolithic Age some six to seven thousand years ago, the Chinese ancients could already dye red sackcloth with hematite powder. Through long-term practice in production, Chinese people had learnt the techniques of dye-extracting and application to yield colorful fabrics. The dyeing techniques came up to a rather high level in the Han Dynasty. There were two major approaches. One is weaving before dyeing, as with thin, tough silk, silk gauze and damask, and the other, dying before weaving, as involving brocade. In the Jin Dynasty, tie-dyeing started to spread among the folk people. By the Sui and Tang dynasties, tie-dyeing became all the rage.

25. Chinese Jade Artwork

Jade has been cherished by the Chinese as a symbol of many virtues. Its hardness suggests firmness and loyalty and its lustre represents purity and beauty. By the middle and late years of the Neolithic Age, jade-carving had been detached from stone ware making to become an independent handicraft. China is a major jade producer in the world. According to Shan Hai Jing (Book on Mountains and Seas), an ancient writing about geography, there are more than two hundred places where jade is found, which means that the source of jade is inexhaustible in China. Hetian of Xinjiang is a well-known place of jade origin in China; Jiuquan of Gansu, Lantian of Shaanxi, Dushan and Mixian of Henan, and Xiuyan of Liaoning are also rich in quality jade resources. Generally, the procedure of jade carving includes jade observation, designing, opening, piercing, cutting and polishing.

第五部分 练习参考译文

22.West Lake Silk Parasol

West lake silk parasol, which is made by bamboo as the frame and silk as the cover, has always enjoyed the reputation of being "the Flower of West Lake". It is light, artistic, stylish and easy to carry. It got its name from the fact that it is made by Hangzhou silk as the cover. As an age-old art, it is believed to emerge as early as the Yellow Emperor period about 4,000 years ago. The parasol industry was thriving in Ming and Qing Dynasty. From then on, parasols were mentioned in many fictions and operas. It is well-known that Xu Xian Borrowed Parasol, one of the plots of the Legend of the White Snake, took place right beside the bridge of the West Lake. This story adds the mythic color of West lake silk parasols. Not only a tool to keep out of the sun but also an elaborate decoration, west lake silk parasol, the perfect combination of practicality and artistry, has become a unique handicraft in China.

23. Chinese New Year Picture

Chinese New Year Picture, known as the picture of "Door Gods" or "Pleasant Picture", is a unique image carrier of the Spring Festival culture. In China, by the close of the year, New Year pictures and couplets are pasted on the external doors of houses to welcome the Spring Festival and drive off the devils and ghosts, enhancing auspicious atmosphere. It is one of the most popular arts among folk people. It will be replaced from year to year and can be appreciated in a whole year, and that is where the name New Year Picture came from. As an age-old art, New Year pictures convey the good wishes of the people for the future, as well as their sentiments and aesthetic tastes.

24. 印染

从天然矿物石和植物中提取染料来染布在中国有着悠久的历史。早在六、七千年前的新石器时代，中国古人就已经会用赤铁矿粉末将麻布染成红色。在长时间的生产实践当中，中国人学会了提取染料并给织物染色的技术。到汉代，染色技术达到了相当高的水平。染色方法主要有两种，一是先织后染，如绢、纱、缎；二是先染后织，如锦。在晋代，扎染开始传到民间。到了隋唐时期，扎染风行一时。

25. 中国玉器

中国人爱玉，将其视为美德的象征。其质地坚硬，代表坚强和忠诚；其光泽晶润，代表纯洁和美丽。在新石器时代中后期，玉雕从陶器制作中剥离出来，成为独立的手工艺品。中国是产玉大国。据《山海经》记载，中国产玉地有 200 多处，足见蕴藏量之大。新疆和田是著名的玉产地。甘肃酒泉、陕西蓝田、河南独山和密县以及辽宁的岫岩也都是盛产美玉的地方。一般来说，玉雕包括选料、设计、做胚、细雕、修整和抛光等工序。

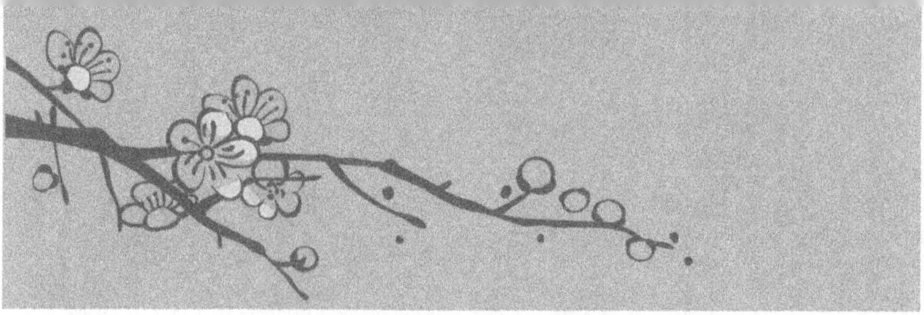

第四章　传统节日

Chinese Traditional Festivals

第一部分 简介

中国的传统节日形式多样，内容丰富，是我国民族悠久历史文化的一个重要组成部分。这些节日的形成过程，也是我国民族的历史文化长期积淀凝聚的过程。我国的传统节日历史悠久，有着极强的内聚力和广泛的包容性，是我国宝贵的精神文化遗产。

Chinese traditional festivals, various in forms and rich in content, are important component of the long history and culture of Chinese people. The formation process of these festivals is also a long-term accumulation and condensation of our Chinese history and culture. These festivals have strong cohesiveness in people and broad inclusiveness, which are valuable cultural heritage of all Chinese people.

第二部分 词汇

Chinese expressions	English expressions
1. 农历，阴历	lunar calendar
2. 阳历	solar calendar
3. 生肖	Chinese zodiac
4. 二十四节气	24 solar terms
5. 烟花	fireworks
6. 爆竹	firecrackers
7. 红包	red envelope
8. 压岁钱	luck money
9. 饺子	dumpling
10. 年糕	rice cake
11. 汤圆，元宵	sweet dumpling
12. 团圆饭	the reunion dinner
13. 灯谜	lantern riddle
14. 祭祀灶神	worshiping kitchen god
15. 舞龙、舞狮	Loong dance / lion dance
16. 民间舞蹈	folk dance
17. 高跷	walking in stilts
18. 龙舟竞赛	loong boat race
19. 纪念	commemoration
20. 艾叶	mugwort leaves
21. 菊花	chrysanthemum

第三部分 文化精选

26. 春节

春节在中国大约有着四千多年的历史，位居中国四大传统节日之首，是中国民间最热闹、最隆重的节日。春节是一种综合性的民俗文化，其中包括祭祀、仪式、节日装饰、饮食和相关的娱乐活动。春节期间的主要活动有：除夕夜包饺子、吃团圆饭和守岁，另外还贴春联、剪纸和放爆竹，正月初一迎神、拜年等。在漫长悠久的历史岁月中，春节从萌芽到定型，不断发展，形成了独具中华民族特色、丰富多彩的习俗。

26.Spring Festival

With more than 4,000 years history, the Spring Festival is the most important festival among four Chinese traditional festivals. It is the most grand and busiest festival in China. As a comprehensive folk culture, it covers many celebrating activities, such as worship, ceremony, festival decoration, food and related entertainment activities. The main activities include making dumplings, and having family reunion dinner on the Lunar New Year Eve, pasting spring festival couplets, making paper cutting and setting off fireworks, as well as New Year greetings and god worship on the first day of the lunar January. In the long history, the Spring Festival has continuously evolved, experiencing a development from the beginning to the maturity. Various customs have been formed with unique Chinese national characteristics.

27. 元宵节

农历正月十五元宵节，又称上元节。元宵节是春节过后的第一个重要节日。中国幅员辽阔，历史悠久，所以元宵节的习俗在各地也不尽相同，其中赏灯、猜谜、吃元宵是几项重要的民间习俗。在一些地区，人们以舞龙、舞狮来庆祝节日。吃元宵是元宵节的一个重要内容。元宵是有馅的糯米团子，代表了满月和人们对于美好生活的希望。

27.Lantern Festival

The Lantern Festival falls on the 15th day of lunar January. Also called as Shangyuan Festival, it is the first important traditional festival and the first big feast after the Spring Festival. China is a large country with a long history, so the customs of the Lantern Festival are different among regions–in right here people celebrate it by watching lanterns, guessing lantern riddles and eating Yuanxiao, while over there people hold lion dancing or loong dancing. Having Yuanxiao is an essential activity of the festival. It is a dumpling ball made of sticky rice flour stuffed with different fillings, representing the full moon and people’s hope for a better life.

28. 清明节

清明节是每年的四月四日或者五日。清明是中国的二十四节气之一，从清明开始气温逐渐升高，降雨增多，这一节气提醒人们应该开始春耕春种了。清明节和农业活动有很密切的关系，在中国清明不仅是季节变换的象征，同时也是一个踏春的日子，最重要的，是一个我们向先人表达哀思的日子。

28.Qingming Festival

Qingming Festival, also known as Pure Brightness Festival or Tomb-sweeping Day, comes on either April 4th or 5th of the Solar calendar. Qingming is one of the twenty-four solar terms of China. From Qingming, temperatures begin to rise and rainfall increases, which indicates that farmers should start to plow and sow. Therefore, the festival is closely related with agriculture. However, in China, Qingming Festival is not only a seasonal symbol, it is also a day for spring outing and, the most importantly, a day for people to show respect to the dead.

29. 端午节

端午节起源于中国，最初是人们祛病防疫的节日。后来传说爱国诗人屈原在这一天投汨罗江而死，于是也成了人们纪念屈原的传统节日。端午节的主要风俗包括赛龙舟、吃粽子、佩戴荷包和五彩线、悬挂艾叶、喝雄黄酒。传说赛龙舟起源于人们划船去救投江的屈原，而佩戴荷包及五彩线则可以保护小孩子远离鬼怪和疾病。

29. Loong Boat Festival

The Loong Boat Festival originated in China, by which people celebrated to prevent epidemic and illness. Later it became a festival for people to commemorate Qu Yuan, a great patriotic poet, who died in the Miluo river on this day according to the legend. The main customs of the loong Boat Festival include loong boat racing, tasting zongzi, wearing a perfume pouch and tying five-colour silk thread, hanging mugwort leaves and drinking realgar wine. Legend holds that the loong boat race originated from the idea that people who rowed their boats to save Qu Yuan after he drowned himself in the river. It is believed that wearing the perfume pouch and tying five-color silk thread can protect children form evil and diseases.

30. 七夕节

农历七月初七是民间的七夕节。古代七夕节最主要的风俗就是女孩子们向织女祈祷有一双灵巧的手，所以又被称为“女儿节”或“乞巧节”。因为风俗的消失和改变，今天的七夕，鲜花和巧克力是最受欢迎的礼物。但是因为牛郎织女美丽的传说，这一天仍然被认为是非常浪漫的节日，也被网络称为“中国情人节”。

30.Double Seventh Festival

The seventh day of lunar July is the Double Seventh Festival. In the ancient days, the most prevalent custom in this day was that girls prayed to a fairy girl called Weaving Maid for skillful hands for sewing, so it is also called"Young Girls' Festival"or"the Begging Festival". Since the traditional customs have been changed and lost, today flowers and chocolate are very popular presents. But because of the beautiful legend about the cowherd and the Weaving Maid, the festival has been endowed with the meaning of great romance, which was also called"Chinese valentine's day"by the internet.

31. 中秋节

农历八月十五是中秋节。中秋节是仅次于春节的第二大盛大节日。这一天的月亮是一年中最大最圆的，所以中秋节又名“月夕”。中秋节也是东亚和东南亚一些国家的传统节日。中秋节的传统活动主要有赏月、猜谜等。中秋节是团圆的节日，也有很多传说和故事，如嫦娥奔月、玉兔捣药、吴刚砍树等。

31.Mid-Autumn Festival

The Mid-Autumn Festival falls on the 15th day of lunar August. It is the second grandest festival in China. Because the moon at that time of the year is unparalleled round and bright, the festival is also called the"Moon Festival". It is a traditional festival for people in east and south-east Asian countries. The common celebration activities on the Mid-Autumn Festival include appreciating the moon and guessing riddles. The festival also celebrates family reunion. There are many legends and stories related to this grand festival, such as Chang E flying to the Moon, Jade Rabbit pounding medicine, Wu Gang chopping laurel tree and so on.

32. 重阳节

九月初九是重阳节。这是一个很古老的节日，形成于战国时期，到唐朝被正式定为民间的节日，距今有一千七百多年的历史了。在中国的数字中，单数为阳，双数为阴，因此九月初九又被称为重阳或者重九。重阳节有很多庆祝活动，比如登高、赏菊、插茱萸、吃重阳糕等。登高是重阳节的习俗，人们认为重阳登高可以避免灾祸，后来逐渐演变成为人们放松心情和锻炼身体的一种形式。1988 年中国政府根据“九九（久久）重阳”蕴含“长久长寿”之意及其风俗习惯，把每年农历九月九日定为“中国老人节”。

32.Double Ninth Festival

With a history of more than 1,700 years, the Double Ninth Festival, formed in the Warring States Period and officially confirmed as a folk festival in the Tang Dynasty, falls on the ninth day of lunar September. Among Chinese numbers, the numbers one, three, five, seven and nine are thought to be Yang (meaning masculine or positive) and two, four, six and eight are thought to be Yin (meaning feminine or negative). Thus, the ninth day of lunar September is called the Double Yang or Double Ninth. The Double Ninth Festival was celebrated by various activities, such as climbing a mountain, appreciating chrysanthemums, wearing cornel and eating double ninth cakes. Mountain climbing is a major custom. Chinese people thought climbing a mountain on this day could help them avoid misfortune and prevent disasters, and later it gradually evolved into a custom for relaxation, hike and exercise. In 1988 the Chinese Government announced the ninth day of lunar September as the "Chinese Senior Citizens' Festival" based on the customs and its implications of "long-lived or everlasting".

第四部分 翻译练习

把下面短文翻译成英语或汉语：

33. 月饼

大多数中国的节日都与特定的食物有关，中秋节也不例外。人们在中秋节吃月饼。月饼是圆的，象征着家庭的团圆，这也就不难理解人们在满月下吃月饼会引起对远方亲友的思念。中秋节家庭团聚，家庭成员拜月、赏月、吃月饼并且表达对远方亲友的思念。

34. 压岁钱

在中国，除夕给小孩子压岁钱的习俗已经有上千年的历史了。除夕之夜晚辈（通常是青少年或者小孩子）向长辈拜年，长辈就会将事先准备好的压岁钱分给晚辈。压岁钱一般放在红色的信封里或者用红纸包着，因为红色是喜庆的颜色。压岁钱代表长辈对晚辈的爱护和希望。相传压岁钱可以压住邪祟，保佑晚辈平平安安度过新的一年。现在孩子们收到的压岁钱越来越多，如何引导孩子合理花压岁钱也就成了一个热门话题。

35. 冬至

冬至，是二十四节气之一，也是中国传统节日之一，是中国的重要节日之一，民间曾有“冬（至）大过年”的说法。古代帝王通常在这一天祭天祭祖，以祈求来年风调雨顺，老百姓则在这一天跪拜父母和祭祀祖先。冬至的习俗南北不同，在中国北方有“冬至馄饨夏至面”的说法，很多家庭在冬至吃馄饨，而南方地区则以吃汤圆为主，因为人们认为汤圆的形状象征着团圆。

36. Laba Porridge

Throughout the history Chinese people have attached great importance to growing crops, so when the land bears a good harvest after a year of hard work, the farmers will show their great gratefulness by sacrificing to the ancestors, and the heaven and the earth. Boiling and drinking Laba Porridge is one of the ways to celebrate the harvest. Laba Porridge is usually made of various rice, beans, dried nuts, lotus seeds, pine nuts and sugar. After centuries of development, there are now over one hundred different cooking methods across the land of China. It is now welcomed by all people of different ages, not for festival food but everyday cooking, because it is easy to prepare, and also so nutritious as a food.

第五部分 练习参考译文

33. Moon Cake

Most Chinese festivals include the taking of particular foods among their customs and the Mid-Autumn Festival is no exception. The Moon Cake is the special food involved here. The Moon Cake is round, which symbolizes the reunion of a family, so it is easy to understand why the enjoying of moon cake in the full moon can evoke longing for distant relatives and friends. On Mid-Autumn Day family members gather to offer sacrifice to the moon, appreciate the bright moon, share moon cakes and express strong yearnings toward family members and friends afar.

34. Lucky Money

The tradition of giving children lucky money on the Chinese New Year's Eve can be traced back to a thousand years ago. On the Eve the young generation, generally the teenagers and children in the family, usually congratulates the old generation happy new year. Then the old generation will give the young some lucky money they prepare in advance. Lucky money is normally wrapped with red paper or in a red envelope, because in China red is the color for joy. Lucky money means the old generation's love and hope to the young. It is believed that lucky money can suppress evil spirits, allowing the young generation to spend the coming year in peace and safety. With the number of lucky money for children to get increasing, how to spend it has been a hot issue for both children and parents.

35. Winter Solstice

Winter Solstice or Winter Festival, one of the 24 Solar Terms, is a traditional Chinese festival. It is so important that there is an old Chinese saying "Winter Solstice is as important as Spring Festival". In ancient times, emperors worshiped the heaven and their ancestors on that day to pray for a good harvest for their people. And common people kowtowed to their parents and offered sacrifices to their ancestors. In north China, the customs of this festival are different from those in the south. There is a famous saying goes in the north of China that "Have dumplings for Winter Solstice and noodles for Summer Solstice", so dumplings are a must for the festival. Sweet dumplings are more popular for locals in southern China whilst. People believe that the round shape of the sweet dumplings symbolizes the family reunion.

36. 腊八粥

自古以来，中国人民就很重视农业生产，因此当一年的辛勤劳动有了丰硕的收获时，农民们会通过祭祀天地祖先来表达感激之情。煮腊八粥也是庆祝丰收的一种方式。腊八粥通常由各种不同的米、豆类、干果、莲子、松子等加糖共同熬煮出来。经过近千年的发展，有近百种不同的煮食方法。今天，腊八粥从节日食品变成了家常粥品，并受到大家的喜爱和欢迎，因为它不仅易于煮熟，而且也是冬天食用的营养食品。

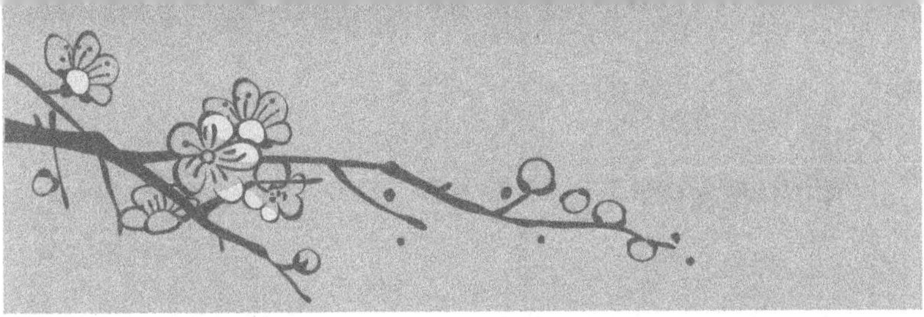

第五章　国学与诗文

Chinese Study and Chinese Poems

第一部分 简介

近代以来，“国学”这一概念泛指中国的传统文化及其研究，包括哲学、历史学、考古学、文学、语言学等，甚至包括中国的古代科学技术，与西方学术界的“汉学”所指内容大致相当。中国的文学作品历史源远流长、内容浩瀚博大，形式极其丰富。本章选取最具有代表性的七方面内容简要介绍中国的国学与诗文。

Since 1840, the term “Chinese study” generally refers to Chinese traditional culture and relevant study, consisting of Chinese philosophy, history, archaeology, literature, and linguistics,etc. even Chinese ancient science and technology included, by which it is close to Sinology, the western academic term. Chinese literature has a long history and it covers so much, and is embodied in various forms. We'll briefly introduce just seven aspects of Chinese study and Chinese poems.

第二部分 词汇

Chinese expressions	English expressions
1. 老子	Lao Zi
2. 孔子	Confucius
3. 孟子	Mencius
4. 庄子	Chuang Zi
5. 《庄子》	Zhuangzi
6. 墨子	Mo Zi
7. 《道德经》	The Classic of the Virtue of the Tao
8. 儒家思想，儒学	Confucianism
9. 道家	Taoism
10. 佛教	Buddhism
11. 阴阳家	Astrologist，Yin-Yang School
12. 哲学的体系	a scheme of philosophy
13. 哲学概念	philosophical conception
14. 哲学思想	philosophy thought/philosophic thinking
15. 学说，教条	doctrine
16. 世界观	world outlook
17. 主观世界	subjective world/internal world
18. 客观世界	objective world/external world
19. 存在	existence
20. 认识	understand

续　表

Chinese expressions	English expressions
21. 反映	reflection
22. 信奉者	adherent
23. 方法和目的	means and ends
24. 原因和结果	cause and effect
25. 宋明理学	neo-Confucianism in the Song and Ming Dynasties
26. 笔画	stroke
27. 天人合一	harmony between the nature and human
28. 宗教	religion
29. 道教	Taosim/Daoism
30. 佛教	Buddhism
31. 佛经	Buddhist scriptures
32. 教义；原则	doctrine
33. 土生土长的	Indigenous/native-born
34. 工匠，手工业工人	artisan/craftsman
35. 孝道	filial piety
36. 国教	state religion
37. 正常的宗教活动	normal religious activities
38. 宗教信仰	religious belief
39. 宗教信仰自由	freedom of religion
40. 象形文字	pictograms/pictographic characters
41. 甲骨文	oracle
42. 偏旁	radical
43. 古代建筑	ancient architecture

第三部分 文化精选

37. 儒家思想

儒家思想（Confucianism）指以孔子为代表所创立的儒学流派。儒家思想是一种社会伦理学与社会管理学，主要从三个方面体现其思想：主张社会和人际关系都应遵守一定的秩序和等级；主张以“礼”“德”和“仁”来管理国家和社会；提倡个人注重人格修养并积极参与社会生活。儒家思想对中国的历史、社会以及个人的思想行为模式都具有深远的影响。

37.Confucianism

Confucianism refers to a philosophical school established by Confucius. In essence, Confucianism is mainly about social ethics and social management. Three aspects mainly embody its proposals: It stresses a certain set of orders and ranks in a society and among people, a principle of “Rites”, “Virtues”, and “Ren” for the management of the country and the society, and it appeals for personal accomplishment and active participation in life. Confucianism exerts a profound influence on Chinese history, society, and personal patterns of thinking as well as behavior.

38. 四书五经

四书五经是四书和五经的合称，是中国儒家经典的书籍。四书指的是《论语》《孟子》《大学》和《中庸》，分别由孔子、孔子门人以及后代弟子所撰。而五经指的是《诗经》《尚书》《礼记》《周易》《春秋》，相传它们都经过儒家创始人之一的孔子的编辑或修改。四书五经对中国社会和汉语影响巨大，比如，《论语》被公认为启蒙教学和修身养性的基本读物，而《诗经》则是中国文学的发端之作。

38.The Four Books and Five Classics

The Four Books refer to Analects of Confucius, Mencius, Great Learning，and Doctrine of the Mean, which were written by Confucius and his disciples. The Five Classics includes Book of Songs, Book of History, Book of Rites, Book of Changes, and Spring and Autumn Annals, which are said to be compiled and revised by Confucius. The Four Books and Five Classics have left deep influence on Chinese society and Chinese linguistics, for example, Analects of Confucius was and is still regarded as a basic book for enlightenment education and self-cultivation, and Book of Songs is acknowledged as the beginning of Chinese literature.

39. 蒙学经典

蒙学经典书籍是指旧时进行启蒙教育时所长期使用的教材。蒙学读物语言简洁精练，读来朗朗上口，作为普通的认知教育读物，易学易懂，方便实用。蒙学读物的内容大都援引自儒学著作，针对儿童的学习特点和认知能力做了改编，并加入了一些自然与社会认知、人生哲学和做人原则的内容，因此对儿童的知识学习、道德教育、言行规范等都非常实用。常用的蒙学经典读物有《唐诗三百首》《三字经》《百家姓》《千字文》《弟子规》等，其中很多内容传诵至今。

39.Enlightenment classics

Enlightenment classics refer to books used for primary education in the long time in ancient China. Although simple and easy, the enlightenment classic books are practical and convenient for primary education. While the main content of those books are from Confucianism classics, they are adapted according to children's acquisition laws and cognitive patterns. Besides, those books were also enriched with common knowledge about science, society, life and morals so as to be instructive for children's education. The most often used books of them include Three Hundred Tang Poems, Three-character Scripture, the Book of Family Names, The Thousand-Character Writing, and Disciplines of Children. Some contents are still read and recited by children today.

40. 汉字

汉字是从原始的象形文字，逐渐演变发展成为一种兼具音、形、意、韵的独特文字。现存中国古代最早的成熟文字是甲骨文。甲骨文也被认为是现代汉字的雏形。此后，汉字的发展又经历了金文、隶书、楷书、草书、行书等不同的阶段。汉字结构“外圆内方”，源于古人“天圆地方”的观念。汉字有五种基本笔画，即横、竖、撇、捺、折。随着中西方文化的交流，汉字已受到许多外国友人的喜爱，形神意蕴的汉字纹身近年在欧洲成为一种时尚。

40.Chinese Characters

Chinese characters were initially meant to be simple pictures used to help people remember things. After a long period of development, it finally became a unique character system that embodies phonetic sound, image, idea, and rhyme at the same time. The earliest mature Chinese characters in ancient times are Oracle，a sort of inscriptions on bones or tortoise shells of the Shang Dynasty, which are also regarded as the original forms of Chinese characters. Afterwards, Chinese characters went through numerous calligraphic styles: bronze inscriptions, official script, regular script, cursive script, running script, and etc. Chinese characters are usually round outside and square inside, which is rooted in ancient Chinese beliefs of an "orbicular sky and a rectangular earth". The five basic strokes of Chinese characters are "—"(the horizontal stroke), "丨"(the vertical stroke), "丿"(the left-falling stroke), "㇏"(the right-falling stroke), and "乙"(the turning stroke). As the cultural exchanges between Chinese and the western, Chinese characters and tattoos with unique shape and meaning has become a fashion by many foreign friends in Europe in recent years.

41. 唐诗

唐诗泛指创作于唐代（618—907）的诗。唐诗是我国优秀的文学遗产之一，也是全世界文学宝库中的一颗灿烂的明珠。唐代被视为中国各朝代诗作最丰富的朝代，因此有唐诗之说。大部分唐诗被收录在《全唐诗》中，而《唐诗三百首》则是流传最广的唐诗读物和蒙学经典。尽管离现在已有一千多年了，但许多诗篇还是广为流传。李白、杜甫、白居易是闻名世界的伟大诗人。

41.Tang poems

Tang poems are generally referring to those written during the Tang Dynasty (A.D.618-907). They are invaluable heritage of China’s ancient literature, so are they sparkling pearls to the world literature. The dynasty of Tang is regarded as one most abundant in poems and that’s why they got the name of Tang poems. Most of the poems are included in Complete Poetry of the Tang, while Three Hundred Tang Poems is the most well-known one. Though written more than ten centuries ago, those poems are still so popular now. Among poets in Tang Dynasty, Li Bai, Du Fu and Bai Juyi are famous to the world.

42. 四大名著

中国的四大名著公认是《三国演义》《水浒传》《西游记》和《红楼梦》。四大名著是中国乃至全人类共同拥有的宝贵文化遗产，在整个华人世界中有着深远的影响。毛泽东说过：“生子当如仲谋，交友如鲁达，信心如唐僧，读书就读四大名著。”研读中国四大名著，是阅历中国古典文学的大海，也是勘察中国传统人文、社会、伦理、历史、地理、民俗、心理、处事策略的知识宝藏。

42.Four Classic (works of Chinese literature)

The most widely acknowledged four classic works of Chinese literature are The Romance of the Three Kingdoms, The Story by the Water Margin, Journey to the West, and The Dream of the Red Chamber, which are the inestimable cultural heritage not only to China but to the world, exerting great and deep influence in the Chinese communities all over the globe. Mao Zedong once said, "Having a child smart as Sun Quan (a character in The Romance of the Three Kingdoms), making friends with one sincere as Lu Da (a character in The Story by the Water Margin), building confidence as Tang Seng (a character in Journey to the West) and reading books as good as the Four Classics". Undoubtedly, reading anyone of the Four Classics is like to surfing on the sea of Chinese classic literature and exploring the treasures of Chinese humanities, society, ethics, history, geography, folklore, mentality, and life philosophy.

43. 中国成语

中国成语是汉语中意义完整的表示一般概念的固定词组或短语。“成语”中的“成”即约定俗成。成语是比词大而语法功能又相当于词的语言单位。绝大多数中国成语由四个汉字组成，如

"自强不息""青出于蓝""厚积薄发"。成语主要从民间谚语、古代文学作品、诗歌、寓言、典故、名言警句等方面提炼而成，是汉语语言中精练而又富有生命力的一部分。寓意深厚的成语充分体现了中华民族的智慧和丰富的历史文化。

43.Chinese Idioms

Chinese idioms refer to comprehensive and integrated fixed phrases and expressions. Idioms are established and accepted by constant usage and common practice. An idiom is a language unit that is larger than a word, but has the same grammatical function as a word. Most Chinese idioms consist of four characters. For example, ziqiang buxi (make unremitting efforts to improve oneself), qing chuyu lan (bluer than indigo), and houji bofa (success comes with time and effort). Idioms are extracted from folk proverbs, ancient works of literature, poems, fables, allusions, and well-known sayings. Idioms are a part of the Chinese language that are concise and have great vitality, fully embodying the wisdom of the Chinese nation and its profound history and culture with far-reaching implications.

第四部分 翻译练习

把下面短文翻译成英语或汉语：

44. 百家争鸣

先秦时期（公元前21世纪至公元前221年），周朝以来的传统价值观逐渐崩溃，思想界呈现百家争鸣的局面。根据汉代官方记载，当时的各种思想流派多达189种，形成了中国哲学的一个巅峰时期。汉代的学者将先秦哲学总结为“百家争鸣”。

45. 网络语言

社会在飞速发展，汉语也随之加快了演变的步伐。网络语言就是汉语进入互联网时代后的产物。或取之于传统媒体（如“中国梦”和“正能量”），或来自外国语言（如“斯诺登”和“江南style”），或产生于网民自创（如“房婶”和“蚁族”），网络语言犹如奔腾不息的潮水，冲击着传统话语方式的堤岸。网络语言大都是“快闪族”，生命力不长久。但也有一些网络语言能经得住时间的考验，登堂入室，被大型词典收录。

第五部分 练习参考译文

44. Contending of 100 Schools

During the Pre-Qin Period (from the 21st century B.C. to 221 B.C.), traditional values from the Zhou Dynasty gradually collapsed, with more than 100 schools of different thoughts contending and flourishing throughout China. According to official records of the Han Dynasty, there are as many as 189 different schools of thoughts at the time, making that period the pinnacle of Chinese philosophy. Scholars in the Han Dynasty summed up the pre-Qin philosophy in "nine genres and ten schools."

45. Network language

The society is developing faster, so is Chinese as a language. Network language is a new product that the Internet has brought to Chinese. Either from traditional media (e.g. "Chinese dream" and "positive energy"), foreign languages (e.g. "Snowdon" and "Gangnam Style"), or from creation of netizens (e.g. "house aunt" and "ant tribe"), network Chinese is pounding on the banks of traditional modes of discourse like surging tides. Though most of network Chinese are "flash mobs" without long-term vitality, some of them can withstand the test of time and be new terms of large dictionaries.

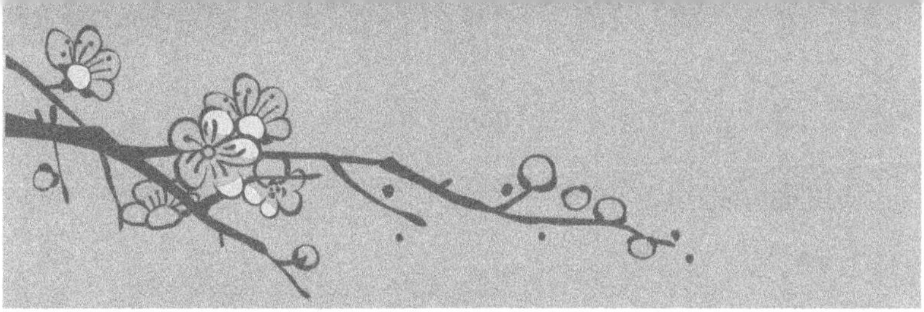

第六章　中医养生
Chinese Medicine & Health Caring

第一部分 简介

中医养生是中国特有的传统医学，是指通过各种方法颐养生命、增强体质、预防疾病，从而达到延年益寿的一种医道之法。中医认为人的身体状况与自然界中的金、木、水、火、土五大元素有关。中医养生重在整体性和系统性，目的是预防疾病，治未病，通过望、闻、问、切来获取中医诊断信息。中医主要从以下三个方面来达到养生目的：天人合一、阴阳平衡和身心合一。

Traditional Chinese Medicine，a unique traditional treatment, refers to enhancing one’s physical fitness, preventing disease and maintaining a joyful life through various methods, so as to achieve a prolong life. TCM views a person’s physical condition as a reflection of the interaction of five elements of nature: metal, wood, water, fire and earth. Holistically and systemically, the goal of Traditional Chinese Medicine is to prevent disease by using the Four Diagnostic Methods of TCM: observation, auscultation and olfaction, interrogation, and palpation. Its health purpose includes three aspects: the harmony between man and nature, the balance of Yin and Yang and the unity of body and mind.

第二部分 词汇

Chinese expressions	English expressions
1. 中医	Traditional Chinese Medicine
2. 颐养生命	maintain a joyful life
3. 增强体质	enhance one's physical fitness
4. 延年益寿	prolong life/Longevity
5. 治未病	preventive treatment of disease
6. 望、闻、问、切	Four Diagnostic Methods of TCM: observation, auscultation and olfaction, interrogation, and palpation
7. 天人合一 阴阳平衡 身心合一	harmony between man and nature the balance of Yin and Yang the unity of body and mind
8. 起源于	stem from/originate from
9. 中庸之道	a middle ground/happy medium/ doctrine of the mean
10. 中和	neutralize/neutralization/neutralizing
11. 辩证唯物主义	dialectic materialism
12. 自发的	initiative/voluntary
13. 医学理论体系	medical system
14. 中医典籍	classics of TCM

续　表

Chinese expressions	English expressions
15. 精髓的	quintessential
16. 生物进化思想	biological evolution thought
17. 临床实践	clinical practice
18. 生物医学疗法	biomedical therapy/Bio-medical Intervention
19. 转换为	convert to
20. 针灸	acupuncture and moxibustion
21. 内病外治	treat an internal illness by external treatment
22. 经脉	meridians
23. 疏通	smooth/ remove obstacles from/eliminate
24. 内脏功能	visceral function
25. 调和	reconcile
26. 捻转	twirling of needle /entwisting / rotating the needle
27. 针刺手法	acupuncture manipulation
28. 艾绒 / 灯芯	moxa/wick
29. 穴位	acupoint /acupuncture point
30. 瘀血现象	congestion phenomenon
31. 拔罐法	cupping therapy /ventouse
32. 非物质文化遗产	intangible cultural heritage
33. 推拿	massage/[中医] manipulation/tuina
34. 崇尚、推行	aAdvocate /uphold/prevail
35. 刮痧	Gua Sha Treatment
36. 毛细血管	[解剖] blood capillary /capillary vessel
37. 汗腺分泌	sweat gland secretion
38. 血液循环	blood circulation
39. 高血压	high blood pressure/[内科] hypertension
40. 中暑	sunstroke /[中医] heatstroke
41. 麻痹	paralysis
42. 调整	adjustment /adjust /modulation

续 表

Chinese expressions	English expressions
43. 经络气脉	meridian nadis
44. 活血化瘀	activating blood circulation to dissipate stasis
45. 清热解毒	clearing away heat and toxic materials
46. 消肿止痛	relieve swelling and pain
47. 调整阴阳	regulating Yin-Yang
48. 协调脏腑	coordination of the internal organs
49. 通行气血	smooth qi and blood
50. 濡养全身	moisten the whole body
51. 生津止渴	help produce saliva and slake thirst
52. 葫芦	gourd
53. 瘀点	petechia (pl. petechiae)
54. 治疗法	remedy/therapy

第三部分 文化精选

46. 中医

中医（Traditional Chinese Medicine）是中国传统医学，起源于中国哲学。中医的“中”是“中和”或“中庸”之意，因此中医就是一门中和的医学。它承载着中国古代人民同疾病做斗争的经验和理论知识，是在古代朴素的唯物主义思想指导下，通过长期医疗实践逐步形成并发展的医学理论体系。中医的基本理论在于阐释生命的自然规律和疾病的变化，主要包括五大理论：阴阳学说、五行学说、养精学说、脏腑（人体内部器官）和经络学说，辨证地论述疾病的缘由，如何诊断和预防疾病以及如何保持健康。

46.Traditional Chinese Medicine

TCM (Traditional Chinese Medicine) originated in Chinese philosophy. TCM is called "Zhongyi" in Chinese, in which "Zhong" means "moderate", or "doctrine of the mean". Therefore it is a moderate medicine. It concludes the experience and theoretical knowledge of the ancient Chinese people when struggling with diseases. With the guidance of the Chinese ancient dialectic materialism, TCM has gradually formed and developed into a theoretical system through long-term medical practice. The principle theory of Chinese medicine attempts to interpret the nature of life and disease changes. Based on five theories: Yin and Yang, the Five Elements, how to direct one's strength, science of zang-fu (internal body organs)and meridians, TCM researches and explains dialectically how diseases occur, how to diagnose and prevent diseases, and how to keep healthy.

47.《黄帝内经》

《黄帝内经》(Huangdi Neijing) 是中国传统医学四大经典著作之一。它是一部为中国医学奠定理论基础和精髓的医学名著，也是中国医学宝库中现存成书最早的一部医学典籍。据传说该书为古代医家托轩辕黄帝 (Huang Ti) 名之作，为医家、医学理论家联合创作，通常被认为成书于春秋战国时期。医著主张不治已病，而治未病，从而达到养生、延年益寿之目的。

47.Huangdi Neijing

Huangdi Neijing is one of the four classics of Chinese traditional medicine. It is a foundation and essence of the theory of Chinese medicine and the earliest extant medical book in Chinese-medicine treasure as well. According to ancient legends, the book was named after Huangdi (Huang Ti) by the ancient physicians who co-worked with the medical theorists in the Spring and Autumn Period. What has been advocated in the book is preventive treatment but not just curing the existing disease for the purpose of longevity and well-being.

48. 中国传统自然疗法

非药物绿色疗法是世界卫生组织提出并在全球推广的一种自然的、安全的生物医学疗法。自然疗法把人与自然结合起来，通过“内病外治”恢复和增强人体活力和免疫力，把体内有害的物质排出体外，达到祛病延年的目的。中国古老的针灸、推拿、气功、刮痧、食疗等传统“绿色疗法”已经走向了世界。自然疗法包括局部疗法和全身疗法。

48.Chinese Traditional Natural Therapies

Non-drug green therapy is a natural, safe and bio-medical therapy, which the WHO (World Health Organization) proposes and promotes. Combining with man and the nature, naturopathies help to regain and enhance the body's vitality and immunity through the way of "treating an internal illness by external treatment". Therefore the harmful substances in the human's can be driven out to achieve the purpose of eliminating disease and prolonging life. Chinese ancient green therapies such as acupuncture, massage, qigong, guasha (scraping), and dietary therapy have been popular in the world for a long time. There are two types of green therapies: local therapy and wholistic therapy.

49. 针灸

针灸是中国医学遗产的重要组成部分，是中国特有的一种古老医疗方法。针灸是针法和灸法的合称。针法是把针刺入患者穴位，通过刺激经络，达到治疗病痛的目的。灸法是以杯罐作工具，把内有燃烧着的艾绒或灯芯的杯罐吸着于皮肤，造成瘀血现象的一种疗法，也称为拔罐法。通过拔罐后皮肤上的罐印颜色可知身体状况。根据中医理论，真空所产生的吸附力有助于排除体内毒素，通经气活气血，从而达到减缓肿痛的功效。

针灸是一门古老而神奇的科学，千百年来一直为广大群众所信赖。2010 年 11 月 16 日中医针灸被列入“人类非物质文化遗产代表作名录”。

49.Acupuncture and Moxibustion

Acupuncture, an old unique therapy, is an important part of the heritage of Chinese medicine. Actually, it is made up of acupuncture therapy and moxibustion therapy. Acupuncture is a way that the operator pierces the needle into the patient's body at a certain acupoint to release pain and treat some diseases by stimulating the meridians; while moxibustion therapy is a treatment that the acupuncturist locates quickly the jar or cup with burning moxa or wick inside on the selected area of the body. This method，as its name is, also known as cupping, can cause congestion in the skin for the cup sucking at a certain point of the surface of it. Acupuncturist predicts and diagnoses the patient's physical state by the color left on the skin after cupping. According to the theory of the TCM, the effect of the suction producing by the ensuing vacuum helps draw out the inner toxins of the body, promotes the flow of "qi" and blood and unblocks channels of meridians to ease swelling and reduce pain.

As an ancient and magical science, acupuncture has been trusted by the masses for thousands of years. On November 16, 2010, acupuncture was included in Representative List of the Intangible Cultural Heritage of Humanity.

50. 推拿

推拿医术是中国古老的医治伤病的方法，是目前中医学的一个组成部分，又称“按摩”。在《黄帝内经》中就提到“经络不通，治之以按摩”的治疗方法。

推拿是指用手在人体的某些疼痛部位或穴位上，按经络、穴位用推、拿、提、揉、捏、点、拍等形式多样的手法对病者身体进行治疗的方法，具有疏通经络、恢复机体功能以及调和阴阳的疗效。它是“以人疗人”的方法，简便无副作用，治疗效果良好，是现在所崇尚的自然疗法的一种。

50.Tui-Na(Massage)

Tui-Na, also known as Massage, one of the oldest Chinese treatments to heal injuries, is an integral part of Chinese medicine. The treatment is mentioned in Huangdi Neijing,“When there is unblocked channels called meridians, Tui-Na will make it.”

Tui-Na is a way of treatment using different techniques by pushing, grasping, pinching, rubbing, kneading and patting with hands on the patient’s meridians and acupuncture points. Tui-Na has the effect of unblocking the meridians, recovering the functionality of the organs, and regulating Yin and Yang of the human body. A humanistic therapy, simple, effective with no side effects, Tui-Na has been prevailed as a natural remedy for present days.

51. 食疗法——广东凉茶

凉茶是岭南（south of the Five Ridges）人民根据当地的气候、水土特性，以中医养生理论为指导，以中草药为基础，研制出的一类具有清热解毒、生津止渴等功效的饮料总称。

广州著名的老字号凉茶店铺有王老吉 (Wong Lo Kat)、黄振龙、金葫芦 (Golden gourd)、徐其修等，各凉茶铺所售的凉茶各有特色，一般都标明自己的品牌。最有名的王老吉凉茶形成于清嘉庆年间（1796—1820），初名王吉凉茶，后改称王老吉凉茶，并沿用至今。

传统凉茶铺的装饰古朴典雅，多在柜台上摆两个葫芦形的大铜壶，凉茶壶也是铜制的，金光闪闪，颇具岭南特色。

51.Food Therapy—Herbal Tea of Guangdong/ Guangdong Liangcha

Herbal tea is generally a kind of beverages in Lingnan District (south of the Five Ridges). Based on the local climate and soil characteristics, and with the guidance of the TCM theory, the people in Lingnan Districts developed such a herbal-based tea, which has the efficiency of detoxification and helping produce saliva and slake thirst.

There are many old well-known herbal tea shops in Guangzhou, like Wong Lo Kat, Huang Zhenlong, Golden Gourd, and Xu Qixiu,etc. all with their own characteristics. They are generally marked with their own brand. The best well-known Wong Lo Kat herbal tea was formed in Jiaqing reign (A.D.1796-1820) of the Qing Dynasty. WongJi herbal tea was named at the beginning, later it was renamed as Wong Lo Kat herbal tea, which has been in use till now.

The traditional herbal tea shop is simply and elegantly decorated, usually with two large gourd-shaped copper pots on the counter. The teapot is also copper-made, glittering and dazzling, which is full of Lingnan characteristics.

第四部分 翻译练习

把下面短文翻译成英语或汉语：

52. 药浴

药浴，在中国已有几千年的历史，据记载自周朝开始就流行香汤浴 (Sweet Shang Yu)。从清代开始，药浴就作为一种防病治病的有效方法受到历代中医的推崇。

药浴在中医中形式多种多样：洗全身浴称“药水澡”；局部洗浴的又有“烫洗”“熏洗”“坐浴”“足浴”等称谓，尤其烫洗最为常用。中医认为通过药物作用于全身肌表、局部、患处，由表及里，可起到疏通经络、祛风散寒、消肿止痛、协调脏腑、濡养全身等养生功效。

53. 刮痧

刮痧是中国传统的自然疗法之一，它是用牛角、玉石等工具在皮肤相关部位刮拭，以达到疏通经络、活血化瘀之目的。在汉语中，“刮”是指用某种工具如牛角在身体的疼痛部位来刮或摩擦；“痧”是指颗粒状的血瘀点，是用来描述在皮下组织血瘀瘀点的术语；刮痧是一种故意引起皮疹或瘀点的自然疗法。中医理论认为刮痧可以扩张毛细血管，增加汗腺分泌，促进血液循环，对于肩周炎、肌肉酸疼、关节疼痛、风寒等都有立竿见影之效。刮痧对机体的作用大致可分为两大类，一是预防保健作用，二是治疗作用。

第五部分 练习参考译文

52. Medicated Bath/ Dipping

Dipping in China has a history of thousands of years. It was recorded that Sweet Shang Yu was popular at the beginning of the Zhou Dynasty. It has been highly praised for its unique effect on the human body from the beginning of the Qing Dynasty.

In Chinese medicine dipping has many forms including wholistic bath called "syrup bath"; and partial bathes as "hot wash", "steaming", "hip bath", and "lavipeditum". In particular, hot wash is most commonly used. Chinese medicine believes that the drug acts on the body from the outside to the inside through the skin surface, locality, and the wounded part. Dipping can clear and activate the meridians, expel cold, ease swelling and pain, coordinate organs, and moisten the body.

53. Guasha

One of the traditional Chinese natural therapies, guasha uses horns, jade and other tools to scrape the relevant parts of the skin in order to achieve the purpose of dredging the meridians and promoting blood circulation. In Chinese, "gua" means to rub or scrape the pain location by using a certain tool, say as a horn. "Sha" is a kind of reddish millet-like petechiae. "Sha" is the term used to describe blood stasis subcutaneous tissue as petechiae. So guasha is a treatment that intentionally raises rash and petechiae. TCM theory holds that scraping can dilate capillaries, increase sweat secretion and promote blood circulation. It has a prompt effect on the symptoms for scapulohumeral periarthritis(frozen shoulder), muscle aches, joint pain and cold. The two main functions of scrapping are namely prevention and treatment.

第七章　传统文体竞技
Traditional Recreation and Sports Activities

第一部分 简介

中国有很多历史悠久、独具特色的传统体育运动。武术就是一项传统的健身项目，比如，太极拳和咏春拳都广受欢迎，爱好者众多。而蹴鞠则有两千五百多年的历史，可以说是现代足球最早的起源。

除传统的体育活动外，民乐在人们的生活中也扮演了一个重要的角色。中国民乐是中国民族乐器和中国民族音乐的统称。中国民乐历史悠久，源远流长，具有鲜明的民族特色。比如，乐器古筝早在两千多年前的秦汉时期就广为流传，而琴曲《广陵散》问世距今已有一千七百多年，对中国文化和民族精神具有深远的影响。

In china, there is a vast variety of traditional sports with a very long history and unique characteristics and attraction. For example, Tai Chi and Wing Tsun are good examples of Chinese martial arts (kung-fu), which are popular among numerous enthusiasts home and abroad. Another example is cuju (also Tsu Chu), which can be traced back to more than 2,500 years ago and be regarded as the earliest form of modern football game.

In addition to traditional sports, traditional music, also, has played an essential role in daily life of Chinese people. The term Chinese traditional music consists of traditional musical instruments and folk music. With a long history, Chinese traditional music has developed with diverse forms and distinctive national characteristics. The musical instrument guzheng (Chinese zithers), as an example, was commonly played during the Qin and Han dynasties more than 2,000 years ago. Guangling San, as a representative masterpiece of guqin (a 7-string Chinese musical instrument), appeared more than 1,700 years ago and has exerted a profound influence on Chinese culture and national spirit.

第二部分 词汇

Chinese expressions	English expressions
1. 文体活动	recreation activity
2. 竞技体育	(competitive) sports
3. 以……为特点	with characteristics of
4. 初具雏形	take shape
5. 打下基础	laid the foundation
6. 越来越大的独立性	increasing independence
7. 被定名为	be named as
8. 日臻成熟	be gradually mature
9. 文化遗产	cultural heritages
10. 刚柔并济	coupling hardness with softness
11. 内外兼修	combining internal meditation with external practice
12. 对生命和宇宙的参悟	deep thoughts on life and the universe
13. 武术，功夫	martial arts, kung-fu
14. 功夫电影	Action film, kung-fu film
15. 太极拳	Tai chi
16. 咏春拳	Wing Tsun
17. 气功	Qi gong
18. 吐纳	deep breathing
19. 中医经络	Chinese medicine meridians
20. 阴阳	Yin-yang
21. 太极八卦	the eight diagrams
22. 以柔制胜	subduing the vigorous by the soft
23. 棋盘	chess board
24. 排兵布阵	the array of troops
25. 楚河	Chu river
26. 汉界	Han borderline

续　表

Chinese expressions	English expressions
27. 棋子	chess pieces
28. 车	rooks or chariots
29. 马	knights or horses
30. 象	elephants or bishops or ministers
31. 士	mandarins or advisors or assistants or guards
32. 将、帅	king or general
33. 炮	cannons
34. 兵	pawns or soldiers
35. 庙会	temple fair
36. 庆典	celebration
37. 粽子	glutinous rice dumplings
38. 祭祀	worship ceremony or fete
39. 竞渡	boat race
40. 民乐	Chinese traditional music
41. 丰富的内涵	enriched connotations
42. 延续并发展	spread and develop
43. 历史悠久	have a long history
44. 源远流长	go back to ancient times
45. 具有鲜明的民族特色	have distinctive national characteristics
46. 民歌	folk songs
47. 起源于	stem from/originate from
48. 民间器乐	instrumental music
49. 曲艺音乐	Chinese folk music
50. 乐器	musical instruments
51. 弦乐器	stringed instruments
52. 打击乐器	percussion instruments
53. 管乐器	wind instruments

续 表

Chinese expressions	English expressions
54. 大珠小珠落玉盘	rapid and soft notes mingled were just like big and small pearls dropping onto the jade plates
55. 春江花月夜	Spring Moonlight on the Flowers by the River
56. 二泉映月	Two Springs Reflect the Moon
57. 古琴	guqin
58. 二胡	erhu
59. 琵琶	pipa
60. 四艺：琴、棋、书、画	the four major arts of China：guqin, chess, calligraphy, and painting

第三部分 文化精选

54. 中国功夫

中国武术即中国功夫，有着几千年的历史，承载着丰富的民族文化内容。作为一项珍贵的中国文化遗产，中国武术讲究刚柔并济、内外兼修，蕴含着先哲们对生命和宇宙的参悟。在现代，中国功夫被功夫大师李小龙首先介绍到美国。功夫电影使中国武术在全世界得以推广。

54.Chinese Kung fu

Chinese martial arts, known as kung-fu, have a history of thousands of years and carry traditional Chinese culture in abundance. As a precious part of China’s cultural heritage, Chinese Kung-fu emphasizies coupling hardness with softness and combining internal meditation with external practice, reflecting creators’ deep thoughts on life and the universe. In modern times, Chinese kung-fu was first introduced to the United States by kung-fu master Mr. Li Xiaolong (Bruce Lee). Kung-fu films have promoted the popularity of Chinese martial arts throughout the world.

55. 太极拳

太极拳是中国传统拳术之一，国家级非物质文化遗产，由明朝初期的道教大师张三丰初创。太极拳以中国传统儒家和道家观念中的太极与阴阳的理念为核心思想，集修身养性、强身健体、技击对抗等多种技能为一体，结合中国传统医学研究成果，是一种内外兼修、以柔制胜、极具传统文化特色的拳术。经过长期演变，太极拳流派众多，爱好者众多。当今，经过标准化整理后，太极拳已经成为正式的体育项目。

55.Tai Chi

Created by Zhang Sanfeng, a Taoist master in the early Ming Dynasty, Tai Chi is a major division of Chinese traditional martial arts and an intangible cultural heritage. Based on the Chinese traditional concepts of Tai Chi and Yinyang from Confucianism and Taoism, the essence of Tai Chi lies in its self-cultivation, physical fitness, and combating. Combining Chinese traditional medicine research, Tai Chi is characterized as physical training, spiritual cultivation and the art of subduing the vigorous by the soft. After long-year evolution, it has become popular with many schools and fans. Nowadays, standardized

Tai Chi has been a formal sport event.

56. 中国象棋

中国象棋的最早记载是在两千五百多年前的战国时代，到宋代时正式成熟，而现在则是中国正式开展的78项体育运动之一，也是第一届国际智力运动会的比赛项目之一。象棋蕴含了《易经》中的精髓思想，体现了中国的古代战争艺术，也发扬了中国传统文化中的“和为贵”的重要理念。象棋在中国几乎老幼皆知，广受欢迎。为促进该项目的普及和推广，2009年，国家体育总局正式将“中国象棋”更名为“象棋”，英文译名采用“xiangqi”。

56.Xiangqi (Chinese Chess)

Firstly recorded in the Warring States period about 2,500 years ago and finally completing its development in the Song Dynasty, xiangqi (Chinese Chess) is now one of the 78 sport events undertaken formally in China and also one item in the first International Intelligence Games. Emboding the ancient Chinese art of war, xiangqi contains and develops the essence thought and concept such as Yinyang in the Book of Changes and “Harmony is precious” in Confucianism. As known by all, young or old, it is popular in China. For the popularization and promotion of xiangqi, in 2009 the General Administration of Sport of China officially announced that “xiangqi” took the name of “Chinese Chess” in English version.

57. 舞龙和舞狮

舞龙和舞狮发源于中国，是中国优秀的传统体育项目，有着浓郁的中华民族特色和悠久的历史文化背景，深受人们欢迎。舞龙、舞狮体现了中国人对民族传统的继承和发扬，因为龙是华夏民族的图腾，而狮子也是中国文化里的祥瑞之兽。可以说世界上但凡有华人的地方，就有舞龙、舞狮的表演。在中国北方，舞龙多见，而在南方，则舞狮流行，无论舞龙、舞狮，都表现了人们在节日庆典时表达吉祥祝福、期盼美好生活的愿望。

57.Loong Dance & Lion Dance

Originated in China, loong dance and lion dance, excellent traditional sports with prominent characteristic of our Chinese nationality and long historical culture, are very popular among Chinese people. They reflect the succession and promotion of the nation tradition, as loong is the totem of Chinese nation and lion, in Chinese culture, an auspicious beast. It has been said that where there are Chinese people, there are loong dance and lion dance. Generally, in the north of China, loong dance is seen mostly while in the south, lion dance is more popular. Either loong dance or lion dance conveys people's auspicious blessing and best wishes for a better life.

58. 赛龙舟

赛龙舟是端午节的一项重要传统。两千多年前，爱国诗人屈原在五月初五投江而死，楚国人划着船去救屈原无果，就往江里投掷粽子来祭奠他。此后每年的这天，人们都会来到江上，缅怀这位尊敬的爱国诗人。最初，赛龙舟仅是一项祭祀活动，现在则演变成了一项传统体育活动。但人们在竞技娱乐之际，并未忘怀赛龙舟的最初目的是为了拯救一位爱国者。

58. Loong boat race

Loong boat race is a major convention in the Loong Boat Festival. More than 2,000 years ago, the patriotic poet Qu Yuan drowned himself in a river on the fifth day of lunar May. At that time, the people of Chu rowed to save him but failed and then they threw zongzi (glutinous rice dumplings) into the river to sacrifice him. Since then, every year on that day people gathered besides rivers or lakes to honor the respectable poet. Originally, it was only a sacrificial activity. Later loong boat race has developed into a traditional sport. However, people never forget the original purpose on that day in boating competition and entertainment.

59. 二胡

二胡是中国传统民族乐器中的弓弦乐器，问世至今已有一千余年的历史。刘天华先生是现代胡琴演奏和琴曲创作的第一人。他改造了二胡的构造，丰富了其表现力，从此使二胡成为一种可以单独演奏的乐器。艺术家华彦钧先生和刘北茂先生创作出了众多的经典二胡作品。华彦钧先生即著名的盲人音乐家，他创作的《二泉映月》可以说是二胡演奏的代表作。作品呈现的是月夜下的诗意景象，表现了创作者对现实生活的忧伤和美好未来的期盼。

59.Erhu

Erhu, a traditional bowed string instrument, appeared more than one thousand years ago. Mr. Liu Tianhua was a master musician who developed modern erhu playing and music composition. He transformed the structure of erhu, enriched its expression and made it a musical instrument that can be used in solo performance. Artists Hua Yanjun and Liu Beimao composed many classical erhu works. Hua Yanjun, a famous blind musician, wrote Two Springs Reflect the Moon, which can be called the representative music of erhu. It conjures up a poetic night scene in the moonlight and manifests the composer's sorrow for the reality and the hope for the bright future.

60. 琵琶

琵琶，得名于枇杷果，已知最早的琵琶出现于秦朝。唐朝时期获得很好的发展，甚至一度在当时的乐器榜上名列榜首，上自宫廷下至普通百姓无不喜爱。现在仍然流行的经典琵琶作品有《塞上曲》《春江花月夜》《十面埋伏》《霸王卸甲》等。著名诗人白居易曾用“大珠小珠落玉盘”这样的诗句来形容琵琶所发出的美妙声音。

60.Pipa

The Chinese traditional musical instrument pipa was originally named after the loquat fruit. The earliest pipa was found to have been made in the Qin Dynasty. By the Tang Dynasty, pipa had developed well and reached its summit on the instruments list. People, from the royal court to the common folk, all enjoyed it. Today, many classical pieces of the pipa are still played, such as Frontier Song and Spring Moonlight on the Flowers by the Rive, Ambush on All Sides, and Conqueror Unarms etc. Bai Juyi, a famous poet of the Tang Dynasty, vividly depicted the wonderful melody of the pipa in his poem: rapid and soft notes mingled were just like pearls dropping onto the jade plates.

第四部分 翻译练习

把下面短文翻译成英语或汉语：

61. 中国功夫电影

作为中国电影史上最负盛名的影片类型，功夫片几乎拥有和中国电影一般长的年龄。早期功夫电影的代表作有《火烧红莲寺》和《黄飞鸿》系列。在 20 世纪 70 年代，李小龙先生把自己的超群武艺和精湛的演技与先进的电影制作技术结合起来，创作了一系列优秀的功夫电影作品，使中国功夫电影和李小龙的名字一样，蜚声世界，也使英语中多了 kung-fu 这样一个新词。李小龙几乎就是中国功夫的代名词。

62. 笛子

在中国，笛子有着非常悠久的历史。大约在四千五百多年前的时候，笛子由骨制改为竹制。在相当长的时间内，笛子曾被称为“横吹”。中国最具代表的笛子演奏曲当为《梅花三弄》，而李白、杜甫等诗人都写过有关笛子的诗句。笛子是中国任何一家民族乐团必备的乐器。笛子在中国非常普及，几乎每个小孩子都会用树枝或者树叶做成笛子玩耍。

63. 编钟

编钟，又叫歌钟，是我国古代的重要乐器，由青铜铸成，依大小顺序挂在木架上。演奏时用木锤敲击，其音色清脆、悠扬，穿透力强。古代用于宫廷雅乐，每逢征战、宴享、朝聘和祭祀都要演奏编钟。1978 年湖北省随县城郊出土了战国初期的曾侯乙墓编钟，共六十五枚，保存完整，被称为我国古代“编钟之王”，至今还可以演奏完整的曲目。

64. Wing Tsun

First popular in provinces of Guangdong and Fujian, Wing Tsun is a southern branch of Chinese Shaolin Boxing. It was originally well-spread in the Yongchun County of Fujian Province, where “Wing Tsun” got its name from the first well-known boxing master, a woman boxer, called Yan Yongchun. Wing Tsun has a set of up close tactics, so it is efficient while the boxer is adjacent to his/her opponents. “Flexibility” is its greatest feature. As a practical boxing for real combat, Wing Tsun embodies the philosophical ideology of traditional Chinese Buddhism and martial arts. The wooden dummy, the well-know token of Wing Tsun, is the important tool for the basic practice of this boxing. Mr. Li Xiaolong (Bruce Lee), “king of kung-fu”, learned Wing Tsun from his master and later created Jeet Kune Do from it.

65. 12-Girl Band

12-girl Band is a Chinese band who plays Chinese folk music in the form of pop music. Established in 2001 in Beijing, 12-girl Band consists of 12 young beautiful national female musicians. Quite different from the traditional folk music playing, they accord Chinese traditional music instruments such as Guzheng, Dulcimer, Pipa, Erhu, Flute, Chinese gourd flute and single-string instrument to play pop music in the fusion of the western pop music elements like Latin, Jazz, and Rock, which makes a wonderful melody. Their unique and passionate performances are greatly appealing to the public. It is a perfect form combination of Chinese traditional instruments and modern pop music, showing the infinite charm of Chinese folk music and the band's innovation.

第五部分 练习参考译文

61. Chinese action (kung-fu) films

As the most prestigious type of Chinese movies, the history of action films is nearly as long as that of the former. The masterpieces of early action films include Firing the Honglian Temple and the Huang Feihong series. In the 1970s, Mr. Li Xiaolong (Bruce Lee) created a sequence of great action films with the combination of his brilliant martial arts, masterly performance and the advanced film production technology. Chinese action films, together with Bruce Lee's name, prevailed all over Asia, America and Europe. As Li Xiaolong became the synonym of Chinese martial arts, a new word "kung-fu" stepped into English.

62. Dizi

In China, the history of dizi (Chinese name for flute) is fairly long. As recorded, more than 4,500 years ago, Chinese people began to make flute with bamboo instead of beast bone. Dizi was once called "side blow" for a very long time. It is believed that the most representative dizi music is Three Variations of the Plum Blossom Tune. Many great poets, such as Li Bai and Du Fu, wrote lines about dizi. Now, dizi is an essential musical instrument for any Chinese folk music band. It is so common in China that almost every child knows how to make dizi with a slim stick or a leaf.

63. Bianzhong

Bianzhong is a set of bells. Also called song bells, bianzhong was an important music instrument in ancient China. Bells are made of cast bronze, and hang on the wooden shelves in accordance with the size of each. Players use a wood hammer to hit on the bells, whose sound is clear, resonant and penetrating. In ancient times, they were played in royal court for feast, worship, ceremony, etc. In 1978, a set of bianzhong with a total of 65 bells were excavated from the Zeng Houyi Tomb of the early Warring States period in the suburb of Sui county of Hubei Province. The set was left intact and can still be played; therefore, it is called “the king of bianzhong”.

64. 咏春拳

咏春拳是中国拳术少林拳之南拳的一个分支，早年流行于广东、福建各地。此拳初传于福建永春县，而且第一位知名的拳师是一位名叫严咏春的女性，所以得名“咏春拳”。咏春拳采用的是近距离战术，贴身攻击能力很强。“灵活”就是咏春最大的特征。咏春拳是一种以追求实战为目的搏击拳术，蕴含着中国佛教和武术的哲学思想。木制的假人是练习咏春拳基本技能的重要工具，也是咏春拳最知名的标志。“功夫之王”李小龙跟师傅学习咏春拳，后来根据咏春拳创立了截拳道。

65. 女子十二乐坊

女子十二乐坊是一个以流行音乐形式来演奏中国民乐的乐团，于 2001 年在北京成立，由 12 位年轻靓丽的民族女乐手组成。有别于传统民乐演奏方式，女子十二乐坊演奏的乐器为古筝、扬琴、琵琶、二胡、竹笛、箫、葫芦丝、独线琴等中国民族乐器，融合西方流行音乐元素的乐曲如拉丁、爵士乐、摇滚等，演奏出独具一格的优美旋律，她们充满激情的表演受到广大民众的喜爱。女子十二乐坊的表演是中国民族器乐与现代流行音乐的完美结合，向世人展示了中国民乐的无限魅力，也显示了乐队的创新性。

第八章　中国名胜古迹

Famous Chinese Sites of Historical Interest

第一部分 简介

中国是古老文明的发源地之一，史料记载已有 5 000 年辉煌的历史。中国古代建筑则是古老文明的一个缩影，已成为世界建筑体系的重要组成部分。勤劳的中国劳动人民创造了许多建筑奇迹，如壮观的地标性建筑——长城，它由西到东蜿蜒 8 852 千米。而紫禁城、秦始皇兵马俑、少林寺和其他众多的名胜古迹则犹如中国历史长河中一颗颗璀璨的明珠。

China is one of the areas where the earliest civilization originated. It has a splendid recorded history of nearly 5,000 years.

The ancient Chinese architecture is a miniature of the civilization, and an important component of the world architecture. The industrious Chinese people created many architectural miracles, such as the Great Wall, the spectacular landmark which winds 8,852 kilometers across the country from east to west. The Forbidden City, Qinshihuang terra-cotta army, Shaolin Temple and many other famous sites are the shining pearls in the long history of China.

第二部分 词汇

Chinese expressions	English expressions
1. 名胜古迹	famous Chinese sites of historical interest
2. 地标	landmark
3. 遗产	heritage
4. 寺庙	temple
5. 古老的	ancient
6. 壮观的	spectacular
7. 朝代	dynasty
8. 综合设施；综合建筑	complex
9. 木质结构	wooden structure
10. 联合国世界遗产委员会	World Heritage Committee of UNESCO
11. 建筑；建筑物	architecture, construction, building
12. 陵墓	mausoleum
13. 以……著称	be famous for/be known for
14. 和谐	harmony
15. 巨龙	gigantic loong
16. 皇帝	emperor

续 表

Chinese expressions	English expressions
17. 等级；级别	rank
18. 步兵	infantry
19. 骑兵	cavalry
20. 为纪念……	in honor of
21. 弟子；徒弟	disciple
22. 做……是值得的	be well worth doing sth
23. 组成	consist of
24. 大规模	large scale
25. 遗址	relic
26. 武术	martial arts
27. 纪念	commemorate
28. 祖先	ancestor
29. 精致的	exquisite
30. 图案	pattern
31. 名人	celebrity
32. 对某人忠诚	loyalty to sb.
33. 居民	inhabitant
34. 东方建筑	oriental architecture
35. 精髓	essence
36. 故宫	the Forbidden City
37. 长城	the Great Wall
38. 秦始皇兵马俑	Qinshihuang terra-cotta army
39. 苏州园林	Suzhou gardens
40. 孔庙	Confucian Temples
41. 少林寺	Shaolin Temples
42. 客家围屋	earthen buildings of Hakkas
43. 莫高窟	Mogao Grottoes
44. 颐和园	Summer Palace
45. 天坛	Temple of Heaven

第三部分 文化精选

66. 故宫

故宫，又名紫禁城，是明清两朝（1368—1911）的皇宫，现为故宫博物院。它位于北京市中心，东西宽 750 米，南北长 960 米，面积达 72 万平方米，共有 9 999 间宫殿，是我国也是世界上目前保存最完整、规模最大的古代皇宫建筑群。1987 年，紫禁城被联合国教科文组织列为世界文化遗产。

66.The Forbidden City

The Forbidden City, called Gu Gong in Chinese and known as the Palace Museum now, used to be the imperial palace during the Ming and Qing dynasties (A.D. 1368-1911). Locating in the center of Beijing, it is 960 meters from north to south and 750 meters from east to west, covering 720, 000 square meters. With more than 9,000 rooms inside, it is the largest and the best-preserved ancient wooden palace complex structure in the world. The Forbidden City was listed as a World Heritage Site by UNESCO in 1987.

67. 长城

长城是古代中国为抵御入侵而修建的防御性军事建筑，始建于春秋时期，有 2 000 多年的历史，秦朝时把所有城墙联结在一起。我们今天所说的长城指的是明朝时重建的长城。它从西到东像一条巨龙，穿过沙漠，越过高山，跨过深谷，蜿蜒而行，最后直到海边，东西绵延上万华里，因此又被称作“万里长城”。长城是世界八大奇迹之一，并被列为世界文化遗产。在北京城区，我们可以去游览八达岭长城。如今，长城不仅对中国人，而且对来自全世界各地的人们来说都是一处名胜。许多人都熟知这句中国名言：“不到长城非好汉。”

67.The Great Wall

As a gigantic defensive military project in ancient China, the Great Wall was built to resist invasion. With a history of more than 2,000 years, it was first built during the Spring and Autumn Period and later was completed during the Qin Dynasty, but the most of it we see today was rebuilt during the Ming Dynasty. Just like a gigantic loong, the Great Wall winds its way across deserts, mountains and valleys from west to east till it reaches the sea. The length is nearly 5 thousands kilometers, so in China it is called the “Ten-thousand-li Great Wall”. The Great Wall is one of the Eight Wonders of the World and is recorded in the World Heritage Directory. In Beijing, tourists can go to visit Badaling Great Wall. Today the Great Wall has become a place of interest home and abroad. Many have come to know the famous Chinese saying “He who has never been to the Great Wall is not a true man”.

68. 秦始皇兵马俑

发现于 1974 年的秦始皇兵马俑位于陕西西安骊山北麓，距秦始皇陵东侧 1.5 千米处。俑坑内共有 8 000 多个真人大小的兵马俑，在地下守护着皇帝的陵墓已超过 2 000 年。他们摆着军阵，犹如时刻准备为保卫皇陵而战斗。每个兵俑的神情、姿势和制服各异，我们可以从中判断出他们或是步兵或是骑兵，甚至还能获悉其军衔。兵马俑享有“世界第八奇迹”的美誉，已被联合国列入世界文化遗产。

68.Terra-cotta warriors

Discovered in 1974, the vaults of terra-cotta warriors are situated in north of Lishan of Xi'an, Shaanxi province, 1,500 meters away from Emperor Qin Shihuang's Mausoleum. Those vaults contains over 8,000 life-size terra-cotta warriors and horses who have been "guarding" the tomb of the emperor Qin Shi Huang, underground, for over 2,000 years. They are arranged in a battle array, showing a readiness for battles to defend the imperial tomb. All figures have different looks, postures and uniforms, by which we can tell from infantry or cavalry, and even their ranks. Terra-cotta warriors enjoy a reputation of "the 8th world wonder" and are listed in the World Heritage Directory by UNESCO.

69. 苏州园林

苏州以其古典园林著称，古语曰：“江南园林甲天下，苏州园林甲江南。”苏州园林以其“天人合一”的设计理念和“巧夺天工”的建筑工艺在全世界享有盛誉。苏州古典园林的历史可以追溯到春秋时期，吴王当时在此修建皇家园林。现苏州城内有超过200座园林，以私家园林为主。沧浪亭（Surging Waves Pavilion）、狮子林（Lion Grove Garden）、拙政园（Humble Administrator's Garden）、留园（Lingering Garden）被称作苏州四大名园，这些园林以精致的设计、一流的工艺和浓郁的文化气息而著称。

69.Suzhou Gardens

Suzhou is especially well known for its classical gardens. There's an old saying "Gardens on the Yangtze Delta are the best, while Suzhou gardens are the best among them". Both for the design concept of the harmony between nature and human and for its ingenious building technology, the gardens have gained a high reputation worldwide. The history of Suzhou classical gardens can be traced back to the Spring and Autumn Period when the emperor of the Wu Kingdom built a royal garden here. Now Suzhou has become a garden city with more than 200 gardens, among which the most are private ones. Surging Waves Pavilion, Lion Grove Garden, Humble Administrator's Garden and Lingering Garden are considered to be the four most famous classical gardens in Suzhou. These gardens are noted for their exquisite design, superb artistry, and cultural content.

70. 孔庙

孔子庙即孔庙，是为纪念孔子为中国文化所做出的重大贡献而建的。孔子是我国伟大的思想家、教育学和儒家学派的创始人，被后人尊为圣人。他一生致力于教育，相传有弟子三千，卓越者有七十二人。孔庙以其宏大的规模、丰富的文化遗产和艺术价值著称。各地的孔庙风格各异，但数孔子故乡的孔庙——曲阜的孔庙规模最大，建造时代最早，它与孔府、孔林并称“三孔”，现已被联合国教科文组织列入《世界遗产名录》。

70.Confucian Temples

Confucian Temples called Kong Miao in Chinese were built in honor of Confucius’ great contributions to Chinese culture. Confucius is a great thinker, educator and founder of Confucianism. Confucius was among the best recognized sages of that period. He devoted his whole life to education. He had some 3,000 disciples and 72 of them were knowledgeable and highly talented. The Confucian temples are famous for their large scales, rich cultural relic collections and their artistic values. The Confucian temples in different places have different styles. Among them, the Confucian temple in Qufu, Shandong Province is the earliest one with the largest scale. The Three Confucius relics—Temple of Confucius (Kong Miao), Cemetery of Confucius (Kong Lin) and the Confucius Family Mansion (Kong Fu) have already been listed in the World Heritage Directory by UNESCO.

71. 少林寺

少林寺始建于北魏年间，位于河南省郑州市的嵩山脚下，是中国佛教圣地和少林武术的发源地。少林寺因少林功夫而名扬天下，号称“天下第一名刹”。少林有习武之传统，古语曰：“天下功夫出少林。”少林寺的文物十分丰富，寺内保存有珍贵的碑碣石刻。少林寺西侧是国内现存的最大的塔林，少林寺塔林是综合研究中国古代砖石建筑和雕刻艺术的宝库。今天少林功夫已成为中华武术的代表，少林文化不仅是中华佛教禅宗文化的独特意象，也是中华传统文化的象征之一。

71.Shaolin Temple

Shaolin Temple was established during the Northern Wei Dynasty, situated at the west foothills of Song Mountain, Zhengzhou, Henan province. It is the home of Shaolin Kung Fu and the holy land of Chinese Buddhism. Known as the best of all the temples, Shaolin Temple is famous for its Shaolin Kung Fu around the world. There is a long tradition of practicing Kung Fu in Shaolin Temple as the saying goes “All martial arts (Kung Fu) are from Shaolin”. Many noted relics locate in Shaolin Temple. On the western side of Shaolin Temple is the largest existing Pagoda Forest in China, which has been a treasure trove to conduct comprehensive study brick buildings and stone carving in China. Nowadays Shaolin Kung Fu has become the representative of the Chinese martial arts. Shaolin culture is regarded as not only a special image of Chinese Buddhist culture but a symbol of Chinese traditional culture.

72. 牌坊

牌坊，也称牌楼，是独具中国特色的建筑，分为木牌楼和石牌楼。它昭示家族先人的高尚美德和丰功伟绩，通常立在坟前、庙前、祠堂前或者路边。牌坊上雕有吉祥的飞禽走兽、精致的花形或名人题字。依功能，牌坊有三大类：一是功德牌坊，记功德，如先人中举，后人会为光宗耀祖的先人立牌坊；二是贞节牌坊，象征节妇对丈夫的忠贞；三是标志坊，没特别含义，只作村或街道的分隔。

牌坊的图案设计主要有龙凤、蝙蝠、鹿和鱼。牌坊上若有龙凤图案的话，通常为皇家牌坊，因为龙是百兽之王，象征着皇帝；凤是百鸟之王，代表皇后。蝙蝠的“蝠”与中文的“福”（祝福）同音，所以，蝙蝠是好运和幸福的象征。鹿与“禄”（收入）同音，意为升官。在牌坊上雕刻“鱼”则寓意会通过重要考试，如科举考试。

72.Memorial Arch

Memorial Arch (Paifang), also called Pailou in Chinese, is a kind of building with unique Chinese characteristics. It is a wooden or stone archway built mainly to commemorate the great achievements or loftiness of family's ancestors. It is often erected in front of a tomb, temple, and ancestral hall or along the road. Many beautiful lucky birds or beasts, exquisite flower patterns, or characters written by celebrities are carved on the arch. Paifang can be divided into three types according to their different functions. The “loyalty” Paifang is used to record a person’s merit or great deeds. If a person passed the imperial examinations, his family members would erect a Paifang because he brought honor to his family. The “chastity” Paifang is built to honor a woman’s loyalty to her husband. Other Paifang s may contain little deep meaning, serving only as a symbol of a street or a village.

The common designs on Paifang include loong and phoenix, bat, deer and fish. The Paifang decorated with loong and phoenix must belong to a royal family, because the loong is the king of beasts and represent the emperor, while the phoenix is the queen of birds and represents the empress. “Bat”, in Chinese, is “bianfu”, with pronunciation similar to “fu” (blessing); so the bat is regarded as a symbol of good luck and happiness. Deer sounds similar to “lu” (salary), signifying promotion. Fish are carved on Paifang to represent the passing of an important test, an imperial examination, for example.

73. 客家围屋

客家围屋，又称土楼，是客家文化中著名的特色民居建筑，被看作东方建筑的奇迹。如今依然有 4 000 座方形、360 座圆形围屋遍布于福建西部的永定县，其数目可谓大得惊人。客家围屋是依照中国文化精髓之“八卦”理念建成方形和圆形，因为古人认为天圆地方。从实用角度来看，客家围屋是防御性建筑，由于客家人居住地大多是偏僻的山区，建筑围屋来抵御野兽或异族。

73.Earthen Buildings of Hakkas

Earthen Buildings of Hakkas (Tulou), famous residential buildings with distinctive features in Hakka culture, are considered a wonder of oriental architecture. Spread around Yongding, in the west of Fujian Province, there are 4,000 square buildings and 360 round ones, which are quite breathtaking. Earthen buildings were created round or square in accordance with the ba gua (Eight Trigrams) theory that the Earth was square and Heaven was round, which was thought to be the essence of ancient Chinese culture. From a more practical point of view, they were built to keep out invaders or wild animals as the Hakkas usually lived in barren and remote hilly environments, they needed to defend themselves from wild animals as well as other clans.

第四部分 翻译练习

把下面短文翻译成英语或汉语：

74. Temple of Heaven

The Temple of Heaven is located in the Chongwen District, Beijing. Originally, it was the place where emperors of the Ming and Qing dynasties held the heaven worship ceremony. It is China's largest and most representative existing masterpiece among China's ancient sacrificial buildings. First built in 1420, it was enlarged and rebuilt during the reigns of the Ming emperor Jiajing and the Qing emperor Qianlong. In 1988, the Temple of Heaven was opened to the public as a park. Its grand architectural style and profound cultural connotation give an insight into the practices of the ancient Eastern civilization, showing ancient philosophy, history and religion of the country.

75. Beijing courtyard

Being a traditional unique folk house in the hutongs, Beijing courtyard has a long history in Chinese architecture. It is called "Siheyuan" in Chinese, "Si" means "four", which here refers to the four sides: east, west, north and south. "He" refers to the surrounding, meaning the four sides circle into a square. Due to its special layout, it is compared to a box with a garden in the center. There is only one gate leading to a hutong, so when the gate is closed it loses touch with the outside world. Therefore family members can fully enjoy tranquility and share the happiness of a peaceful family union.

76. Lijiang Old Town

The Old Town of Lijiang, a well-preserved old city of ethnic minorities with brilliant culture, is a central town of the Lijiang Autonomous County of the Naxi Ethnic Minority in Yunnan Province. Located on the plateau which is 2,400 meters above the sea level and embraced by the tree-covered Lion Mountain in the west, Elephant and Golden Row Mountains in the north, vast fertile fields in the southeast and crystal clear water running through, the old town looks like a big jade ink slab, therefore got the alias the Town of Big Ink Slab (Dayanzhen). With a long history, the Ancient Town of Lijiang features primitive simplicity, naturalness and a wonderful urban mosaic of mountainous city scenery and water county style. Folk dwellings in Lijiang integrate the finest traditions of different nationalities and bear the unique style of Naxi people, forming a rare legacy for the study of Chinese architectural and cultural histories.

77. 敦煌莫高窟

莫高窟（Mogao Grottoes）俗称千佛洞，被誉为 20 世纪最有价值的文化发现。坐落在河西走廊西端的敦煌，以精美的壁画和塑像闻名于世，现有洞窟 492 个，壁画 4.5 万平方米， 泥质彩塑 2 415 尊，由南向北横跨 1 600 米，是世界上现存规模最大、内容最丰富的佛教艺术圣地。1987 年，莫高窟被联合国教科文组织列为世界文化遗产。

78. 颐和园

颐和园位于北京市海淀区，距北京中心城区 15 千米，是中国现存规模最大、保存最完整的皇家园林。它以其著名的自然景观和人文景观极大地影响着中国的园艺和园林艺术，很早就被誉为“皇家园林博物馆”。颐和园始建于 1750 年，最初是供皇室成员休闲和娱乐的奢华的皇家园林，后来在清末成为皇室成员的主要住所。

第五部分 练习参考译文

74. 天坛

天坛，位于北京市东城区，最初是明清两代皇帝祭天之地。它是中国现存最大、最具代表性的古代祭祀建筑杰作。天坛始建于 1420 年，在明朝嘉靖和清朝乾隆年间得以扩建和改建。1988 年天坛被辟为开放公园。其宏伟的建筑风格和深厚的文化内涵反映了中国古代的哲学、历史和宗教信仰，可以让人们深刻了解古代东方文明。

75. 四合院

北京四合院是胡同里一种传统的独特民居，在中国建筑史上有着悠久的历史。中文的汉语拼音为“Siheyuan”，“si”对应的汉字是“四”，在这里指的是四个方向：东、西、南、北。“he”对应的汉字是“合”，汉语意思是“围绕”，即四边围成一个方形。由于其独特的布局，它好比是一个中心为花园的盒子。由于四合院只有一个门通向胡同，因此，一旦把门关上，它就与外面的世界隔绝，这样一家人就可以充分独享宁静和团圆的幸福。

76. 丽江古城

丽江古城，一座保存完好的老城，其闪烁着灿烂的少数民族文化，是云南丽江纳西族自治县的城镇中心。位于海拔 2 400 米的高原上，西枕绿树环绕的狮山，北依象山和金虹山，东南面临数十里的良田沃野，一片碧野之间绿水萦绕，因而使这座古城看上去形似一块碧玉大砚，故又被称作“大研古镇”(古时“砚”和“研”相通)。丽江古城历史悠久，古朴自然。城市布局错落有致，既具有山城风貌，又富于水乡韵味。丽江民居既融和了各民族精华，又有纳西族的独特风采，是研究中国建筑史、文化史不可多得的重要遗产。

77. Mogao Caves

The Mogao Caves are commonly known as the Thousand-Buddha Caves and considered to be the most valuable cultural discovery in the 20th century. Located in Dunhuang in the west of Hexi corridor, the Mogao Caves are famous for their beautiful murals and statues. There are 492 caves, 2,415 sculptures and 45,000 square meters of murals at the site, which spans 1,600 meters from north to south. Being the largest and richest shrine of Buddhist art treasures in the world, the Mogao Caves were listed in the World Heritage Directory by UNESCO in 1987.

78. Summer Palace

Situated in the Haidian District, Beijing, the Summer Palace is 15 kilometers from the downtown area of Beijing. As the largest and most well-preserved royal park in China, it greatly influences Chinese horticulture and landscape design with its famous natural views and cultural interests, and it also has long since been recognized as "The Museum of Royal Gardens". The construction started in 1750 as a luxurious garden for royal families to rest and entertain. In the end of the Qing Dynasty it became the main residence of royal members.

第九章　中国饮食文化

Chinese Food Culture

第一部分 简介

俗话说，民以食为天。在中国，无论是喧嚣的都市，还是偏远的小镇，都能找到独具特色的地方美食，或麻辣咸香，或清爽酥脆，总让人回味无穷。中国人讲究吃，不仅仅是一日三餐、解渴充饥这么简单，往往还蕴含着中国人认识事物、理解事物的哲理。四季有别、讲究情趣、注重美感、食医结合是中国饮食文化的四个主要特点。

There is an old saying: food is the first necessity of people. In China wherever you go, no matter where it is a metropolis or a remote town, you can always find some special local food. With rich or subtle tastes, they leave people memorable experiences. Implying some philosophy on recognizing and understanding the world, food, for Chinese, is more than three meals a day, or assuaging one's hunger. The food choice in different seasons, the attention to delight in food, the care for the appearance of food, and the combination of food and therapy, are considered as the four main features of Chinese food culture.

第二部分 词汇

Chinese expressions	English expressions
1. 民以食为天	Food is the first necessity of people
2. 解渴充饥	to assuage one's hunger and thirst
3. 哲理	philosophy
4. 情趣	delight
5. 食医结合	the combination of food and therapy
6. 小吃店 / 小吃摊	snack bar/stand
7. 吃货	foodie
8. 审美标准	the aesthetic standards
9. 宫廷菜	the imperial dishes
10. 地方风味	local flavor
11. 蒸，烧，炖，炒，煎	steaming, braising, stewing, stir-frying，frying
12. 麻辣	spicy and hot
13. 酸辣	sour and hot
14. 刀工严谨	good cutting skills
15. 玲珑	exquisite
16. 礼仪	etiquette

续　表

Chinese expressions	English expressions
17. 礼仪之邦	a state of ceremonies
18. 座次	the order of seats
19. 吃相	eating manners
20. 行为规范	behavioral norms / codes of conduct
21. 天人合一	harmony between heaven and human
22. 群体意识	sense of community
23. 火锅	hot pot
24. 铜鼎	bronze tripod
25. 前身	predecessor
26. 出土文物	unearthed relics
27. 斗	bucket
28. 钙骨火锅	chop hot pot
29. 肥腻	greasy
30. 吊人口胃	whet the appetite
31. 羊肉涮锅	lamb shabu
32. 吃货	gourmand/foodie
33. 营养	nutrition
34. 柴	firewood
35. 酱油	soy sauce
36. 醋	vinegar
37. 饮料	beverage
38. 砖茶	brick tea
39. 花茶	scented tea
40. 达官贵人	dignitary
41. 平民百姓	ordinary folk
42. 罪魁祸首	culprit
43. 修身养性	nourish one’s inborn nature

续 表

Chinese expressions	English expressions
44. 广式早茶	Cantonese morning tea
45. 点心	Dim Sum
46. 其乐融融	enjoyable
47. 亲朋好友	friends and relatives
48. 敬酒	toast
49. 红酒	red wine
50. 白酒	liqueur
51. 黄酒	yellow wine
52. 料酒	cooking wine
53. 肥而不腻	flesh abundance without greasy
54. 肉质细嫩	tender meat
55. 口味鲜美	delicate
56. 酥脆	crispy

第三部分 文化精选

79. 八大菜系

由于气候环境、文化传统和民族习俗等差异，中国菜式形成了以鲁菜、川菜、粤菜、闽菜、徽菜、苏菜、浙菜、湘菜为代表的八大菜系。这八大菜系各有特点：鲁菜大方古朴，口味鲜美纯正，符合儒家的审美要求，是古代的宫廷菜；川菜以麻辣著称，地方风味极为浓厚；粤菜发源于岭南，用料广、博、杂，是国外中国菜的代表；闽菜选料精细，刀工严谨，色调美观；徽菜主要流行于浙江西部和徽州地区，擅长烧炖，常以火腿佐味，冰糖提鲜；此外，苏菜口味趋甜；浙菜玲珑秀丽；而以鲜、香、酸、辣闻名的湘菜则油重色浓，号称民间第三大菜系（第一和第二分别是川菜和粤菜）。

79.Eight Major Cuisines of China

The diversity of climate, geography, culture and custom gave birth to eight main cuisines, which are representative of Chinese food. They are as follows: Shandong Cuisine, Sichuan Cuisine, Guangdong (Canton) Cuisine, Fujian Cuisine, Huizhou Cuisine, Jiangsu Cuisine, Zhejiang Cuisine and Hunan Cuisine. Distinctive and typical, the eight cuisines have their own features: with pure flavor and elegant appearance, Shandong Cuisine satisfies the aesthetic standards of Confucianism, which was the representative of the imperial dishes of China. Sichuan Cuisine is famous for its spicy and hot flavor, which has strong regional characteristics. Originated from Guangdong, characterized by diverse and rich food resources, Cantonese Cuisine is the most influential Chinese food outside of China. Fujian Cuisine focuses on choosing superior food resources, having beautiful colors and showing good cutting skills. Huizhou Cuisine is popular in the west of Zhejiang Province and Huizou district, which is good at braising and stewing, while hams and sugar candy are added to improve the fresh taste. Jiangsu Cuisine tends to show its preference for sweet flavor, while Zhejiang Cuisine is exquisite and beautiful. Famous for being sour and hot, delicious and savory, Hunan Cuisine strikes people as thick-oiled and Chili-colored, which is called the third Cuisine among Chinese folk (by the way, the first is Sichuan Cuisine and the second is Cantonese Cuisine).

80. 餐饮礼仪文化

中国自古为礼仪之邦，早在周代就已经形成了一套相当完善的饮食礼仪制度。这些饮食礼仪，经过以孔子为代表的儒家先哲们的补充完善，在中国古代社会发挥过重要作用，对现代社会也产生着不小的影响。传统的餐饮礼仪包括宴饮之礼、待客之礼、进食之礼，对座次、吃相等有着严格的规定，是文明社会的重要行为规范。

随着中国的对外开放，传统的中国餐饮礼仪开始和西方餐饮礼仪相融合，虽已化繁就简，但仍保留了以下特征：

（1）注重天人合一。很多盛大的节日与饮食有关，如元宵节吃元宵、端午节吃粽子、中秋节吃月饼等。

（2）强调群体意识，追求团结和团圆。这主要表现在：第一，除夕夜吃团圆饭，是中华民族几千年的传统；第二，偏爱圆桌和圆形的食物。在汉语中，圆形象征着团圆，而圆桌也可以坐更多的人，便于面对面地交流。

80.Dining Etiquette Culture

China has been a state of ceremonies since the ancient time, as a whole set of dining etiquette system developed as early as in Zhou Dynasty. Having been supplemented and perfected gradually by

Confucian sages, these etiquettes played an important role in ancient Chinese society. Moreover, they are also influencing the modern society. Traditional dining etiquettes include the manners on feasting, treating, and eating, which had strict regulations on the seating arrangement, eating manners, etc., and became important codes of conduct in civilized society.

With the opening-up of China, traditional Chinese dining etiquette has been combined with the western's, from complicated to simple, but remains the following features:

(1) Stressing the harmony between the heaven and the human. What the most remarkable is: food is relative to many big festivals. For example, people will have sweet dumplings in the Lantern Festival, zongzi in the loong Boat Festival, moon cakes in Mid-autumn Festival, etc.

(2) Emphasizing the sense of community, chasing solidarity and reunion. This is reflected in the following aspects: firstly, Chinese will try to go back for a big family reunion dinner on New Year's Eve, which lasts thousands of years as one of Chinese traditional customs. Secondly, Chinese people like round tables and round food. "Round" means "reunion" in Chinese, and the round tables are capable of containing more people. Among others, they are also convenient for people to communicate face to face.

81. 火锅

关于中国火锅的起源，有两种说法：一种说其源于三国或隋朝，那时的“铜鼎”就是火锅的前身；另一种说法是，火锅始于东汉，出土文物中的“斗”指的就是火锅。由金属或陶瓷制成的锅置于炉上，使锅汤常沸以熟菜肴，随煮随吃。作为民间流行的美食，因地区不同而各具特色，可谓百锅千味。著名的有：重庆的麻辣火锅，麻辣醇香，名扬天下；广东的海鲜火锅、钙骨火锅食而不腻，味美无穷；北京的羊肉涮锅风味别致，吊人胃口。寒冬里围聚一锅热气腾腾的火锅，实为亲朋好友聚会的不错选择，不仅大饱口福，还能增进感情。

81.Hot pot(Chafing Dish)

There are two versions of the origin of Chinese hot pot: one is said to date back to the Three Kingdoms or the Sui Dynasty, when the “bronze tripod” is the predecessor of hot pot; another argument is from Han, where relics of the “bucket” is said to be the pot. Metal or ceramic-made pot is placed on the stove for people to put what they like to eat into the boiling soup and take them. As a popular folk cuisine, hot pot dishes have diverse tastes and styles varying from region to region. The well-known types are as Chongqing hot pot with spicy mellow, Guangdong Seafood hot pot and chop pot with fresh and taste without greasy, and Beijing Lamb shabu with unique flavor whetting the appetite. It is really a good choice to have a hot pot meal with friends or relatives in the cold winter, where people can not only have a big treat, but also enhance the friendship and ties.

82. 茶文化

作为世界三大饮料之一，茶在中国的历史已经超过了 4 000 年。据说，中国是茶的故乡，是世界上最早发现茶树、栽培茶树的国家之一。中国有句俗语：开门七件事，柴米油盐酱醋茶。茶已经成为人们生活中不可缺少的一部分。无论是达官贵人，还是市井百姓，都对茶情有独钟。品茶也成为一种独特的中国文化。通过赏茶和品茶，人们不仅可以修身养性，还可以增进友谊。我国的茶叶品种主要有红茶、绿茶、乌龙茶、砖茶、花茶等。

82.Tea Culture

Tea is one of the three soft drinks in the world. With a long history of more than 4,000 years, China is regarded as the hometown of tea. Besides, China is also one of the countries where people first found the tea shrubs and cultivated them. As a Chinese old saying goes, firewood, rice, oil, salt, sauce, vinegar and tea are the seven necessities to begin a day. Not only the dignitaries but also ordinary folks show special preference to tea, so it has become an indispensable part of daily life. Tasting tea is also a unique culture of China. Through appreciating and tasting tea, people can nourish their inborn nature and promote friendship among each other. Black tea, green tea, oolong tea, brick tea, and scented tea are the main varieties of tea in China.

83. 广式早茶

喝早茶是广东传统文化的重要组成部分，其实质就是去餐馆吃早餐。喝早茶也是广东人一种通常的社交方式。亲朋好友，约上茶楼，饮茶品点，谈心叙谊，其乐融融。不少人洽谈业务、协调工作，甚至谈情说爱，也喜欢用喝（早）茶的方式进行，这也是喝早茶的风尚能长盛不衰甚至更加延伸扩展的缘由。

83.Cantonese Morning Tea

Drinking morning tea is a big part of Cantonese traditional culture. Actually it means having a breakfast in restaurants. It's enjoyable to chat with a couple of friends or relatives while having a cup of tea and Dim Sum in restaurants. Cantonese consider it as a common-used method of social intercourse. Some people treat morning tea for business, coordination or dating, which is why morning tea can last long and even be extended.

84. 酒文化

在几乎所有的重要场合，人们都要喝酒以示庆祝。 酒文化因此也成为中国传统文化中不可替代的一个重要组成部分。 中国人对酒有着复杂的感情，不少成语诗句都与之相关，如“借酒浇愁”“酒逢知己千杯少”等。然而，酒也是车祸等惨剧的罪魁祸首，所以，很多公益组织不断呼吁适度饮酒的文明生活方式。

84.Wine culture

Nearly all important occasions are celebrated with alcohol, for which the alcohol culture becomes an important and indispensible component of Chinese culture. Chinese have a mixed feeling on alcohol, which was expressed in some Chinese idioms or poems："酒逢知己千杯少"（When drinking with a bosom friend , a thousand cups will still be too little），"借酒浇愁"（drown one's sorrows），and etc.

However, alcohol is the culprit of many tragedies like traffic accidents. Therefore, the propaganda of drinking with measure as a civilized way of life has been being a repeated topic of various non-interest groups.

第四部分 翻译练习

把下面短文翻译成英语或汉语：

85. Chinese Cuisine

Many people like Chinese cuisine. In China, it is not only regarded as a craftsmanship, but also an art. An exquisitely prepared Chinese cuisine is a feast for both the mouth and the eyes. The culinary skill and dish ingredients vary in different regions of China, but good Chinese cuisines always have something in common, i.e. the color, aroma, taste and nutrition. As food is vital for one's health, a good chef always tries to keep a balance among grains, meat and vegetables. That's why Chinese cuisine is delicious and healthy.

86. Beijing Roast Duck

Beijing roast duck, one of the famous Chinese dishes, claret color, tender meat, mellow taste, and greasy yet agreeable, has won fame both at home and abroad. It is said that Premier Zhou Enlai greatly appreciated and kept concern to this dish, with which he entertained the foreign guests.

Beijing roast duck is divided into two major schools—the "Quanjude" and the "Pianyifang". Hanging on the burning furnace, which uses some fruits trees (such as date and pear wood) as fuel, "Quanjude" roast duck has a unique taste with fruit fragrance with thin crispy, ruddy color, and abundant flesh but without greasy. While stewed in a "stew stove" made of bricks, in which the charcoal is grilled, roast duck in the "Pianyifang" looks oily with crispy skin, fleshy white and delicate taste. In contrast, stewed stove duck tastes much tender and more abundant with some duck juice, hanging furnace duck perhaps shows you more wisdom of the earliest human use of "roast" cooking method.

87. 饮酒礼仪

中国的饮酒礼仪体现了对饮酒人的尊重。谁是主人、谁是客人，都有固定的座位。关于敬酒的顺序也有说法：敬酒时要从主人开始，主人不敬完，别人是没有资格敬的，如果乱了次序是要"受罚"的。而西方人饮用葡萄酒的礼仪，则反映出对酒的尊重。

88. 茶还是咖啡？

“你要茶还是咖啡？”是用餐人常被问到的问题，许多西方人会选咖啡，而中国人则会选茶。相传，中国的一位帝王于五千年前发现了茶，并用来治病。在明清 (the Ming Dynasty and Qing Dynasty) 期间，茶馆遍布全国。饮茶在 6 世纪传到日本，但直到 18 世纪才传到欧美，如今，茶是世界上最流行的饮料 (beverage) 之一。茶是中国的瑰宝，也是中国传统文化的重要组成部分。

第五部分 练习参考译文

85. 中餐

许多人喜欢中餐。在中国，烹饪不仅被视为一种技能，而且也被视为一种艺术。精心准备的中餐既可口又好看。烹饪技艺和配料在中国各地差别很大，但好的烹饪都有一个共同点，总是要考虑到颜色、味道、口感和营养 (nutrition)。由于食物对健康至关重要，好的厨师总是努力在谷物、肉类和蔬菜之间取得平衡，所以中餐既味美又健康。

86. 北京烤鸭

北京烤鸭是具有世界声誉的著名汉族菜式，它以色泽红艳、肉质细嫩、味道醇厚、肥而不腻的特色，被誉为“天下美味”而驰名中外。据说周总理生前十分欣赏和关注这一名菜，宴请外宾，品尝烤鸭。

北京烤鸭分为两大流派——“全聚德”和“便宜坊”。“全聚德”采用的挂炉烤鸭因以枣木、梨木等果木为燃料，用明火，故其味带有果木清香，皮薄香脆，色泽红润，肉质肥而不腻。以“便宜坊”为代表的焖炉烤鸭采用“焖炉”即地炉，炉身用砖砌成，由炉内炭火和烧热的炉壁焖烤而成，因其制作时不见明火，使得焖炉烤鸭外皮油亮酥脆，肉质洁白、细嫩，口味鲜美。相比而言，焖炉烤鸭口感更嫩一些，鸭皮的汁也明显更丰盈饱满些，而挂炉烤鸭似乎更能让人体会到人类最早掌握的“烤”的烹饪方法的智慧。

87. Drinking etiquette

The Chinese etiquette in drinking shows the respect for the drinkers. The host and the guests have their fixed seats. Customs about toasting order should be noted: toasting is supposed to start with the host, the others are not entitled to toast before the host. People will be “punished” for the disorder of toasting. In contrast, the western people show their respect for the wine while drinking.

88. Tea or coffee？

“Tea or coffee?” Diners are often asked this question. Many western people may choose coffee, while Chinese may prefer tea. It is said that 5,000 years ago, an emperor in China discovered tea and used it to cure disease. During the Ming Dynasty and Qing Dynasty, tea houses could be found all over the country. Tea-drinking was introduced to Japan in the sixth century, but was not introduced to

Europe and America until the 18th century. Now, tea is one of the most popular beverages in the world. It is the national drink of China and an important part of Chinese traditional culture.

第十章 其他

Others

第一部分 简介

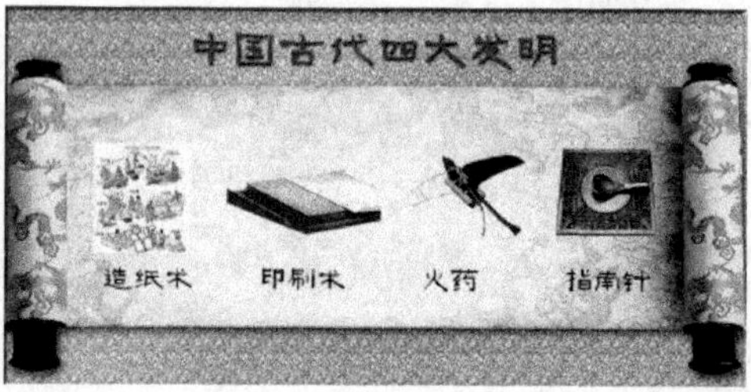

中国文化博大精深，所涵盖的内容远不止前面几章提到的那些，有些内容很难将其列入所属范畴，很多方面难以顾及。本章主要介绍中国的龙文化、婚嫁习俗、二十四节气、十二生肖和四大发明，权作拾遗。

Extensive and profound, Chinese culture is more than what have been mentioned above, because some aspects of Chinese culture are not so easy to be classified as what is done in previous chapters. As a complement, this chapter mainly introduces loong, wedding customs, the 24 solar terms, 12 Chinese zodiacs, and the four great inventions of ancient China.

第二部分 词汇

Chinese expressions	English expressions
1.（中国）龙	(China) Loong (not western dragon)
2. 罪魁祸首	culprit
3. 炎黄子孙	Chinese nation/people, descendants of Yan and Huang
4. 婚俗	wedding customs
5. 说媒	matchmaking
6. 求亲	proposal
7. 定亲	engagement
8. 聘礼	betrothal gifts
9. 嫁妆	dowry
10. 迎娶	wedding ceremony
11. 拜堂	performing ritual kneeling in wedding
12. 交杯酒	cross cupped wine，wedlock wine
13. 闹洞房	celebrate wedding in bridal chamber
14. 礼仪	etiquette
15. 敬酒	toast
16. 节气	Solar terms
17. 立春	Start of Spring (1st solar term)
18. 雨水	Rain Water (2nd solar term)
19. 惊蛰	Awakening of Insects (3rd solar term)
20. 春分	Spring Equinox (4th solar term)
21. 清明	Clear and Bright (5th solar term)
22. 谷雨	Grain Rain (6th solar term)
23. 立夏	Start of Summer (7th solar term)
24. 小满	Grain Buds (8th solar term)
25. 芒种	Grain in Ear (9th solar term)

续 表

Chinese expressions	English expressions
26. 夏至	Summer Solstice (10th solar term)
27. 小暑	Minor Heat (11th solar term)
28. 大暑	Major Heat (12th solar term)
29. 立秋	Start of Autumn (13th solar term)
30. 处暑	End of Heat (14th solar term)
31. 白露	White Dew (15th solar term)
32. 秋分	Autumnal Equinox (16th solar term)
33. 寒露	Cold Dew (17th solar term)
34. 霜降	Frost's Descent (18th solar term)
35. 立冬	Start of Winter (19th solar term)
36. 小雪	Minor Snow (20th solar term)
37. 大雪	Major Snow (21st solar term)
38. 冬至	Winter Solstice (22nd solar term)
39. 小寒	Minor Cold (23rd solar term)
40. 大寒	Major Cold (24th solar term)
41. 历法	calendar
42. 生肖	zodiac
43. 指南针	compass
44. 火药	gunpowder
45. 造纸术	paper making techniques
46. 印刷术	printing techniques
47. 炼丹家	alchemists
48. 军事家	militarist
49. 雕版印刷	woodblock printing
50. 活字印刷	typography
51. 母系氏族制	the matriarchal society
52. 血统、氏	lineages

续　表

Chinese expressions	English expressions
53. 神农	Shen Nong
54. 图腾	totem
55. 谥号	the posthumous title
56. 少数民族	minorities
57. 忌讳、禁忌	taboo
58. 好事成双	Good things go in pairs
59. 吉利	auspicious/lucky
60. 送终	burying a senior member
61. 羁绊	fetter

第三部分　文化精选

89. 龙文化

与西方文化中龙（dragon）的邪恶印象不同，对每一个炎黄子孙来说，龙是中华民族的象征，意味着尊严和力量，是实现人们愿望的天使。龙并不是一种实际存在的动物，而是几种动物的混合体。随着时代的变迁，龙的形象日趋完美，也变得无所不能，各种代表着人们的美好愿望的成语层出不穷，如“龙马精神”“龙凤呈祥”“卧虎藏龙”“望子成龙”等。“龙的传人”已成为中国人在世界的代名词。

89.Loong Culture

Different from the malevolent image of western Loongs, Loong, the symbol of Chinese nation in Chinese represents dignity and power, an angel who helps fulfill people's wishes. Loong image rooted in Chinese is not a real animal, but a combination of some animals which people were familiar with. The image of Chinese Loong has undergone a series of changes over the centuries and becomes more and more mighty and beautiful. Many Chinese idioms formed with Loong have emerged, such as "龙马精神", "龙凤呈祥", "卧虎藏龙", "望子成龙", representing people's good expectations. The term of "descendents of Loong" has become a synonym for Chinese people in the world.

90. 婚俗

中国传统婚俗一般指的是汉族的婚礼习俗，它包括七个必备步骤：说媒、定亲、聘礼、迎娶、拜堂（三鞠躬）、交杯酒、闹洞房。这些习俗源于中国几千年的文化积累，几乎每一项礼仪都渗透着中国传统的哲学思想。虽然有些已被现代人淡忘或忽略，但其根本依然或多或少的影响着人们。如红色在汉语中象征着美好和喜庆之意，因此在现代婚礼中人们仍然沿袭了着红衣、穿红鞋、贴红囍、盖红被等传统习俗；在新人床上撒上红枣、花生、桂圆、莲子（代表着早生贵子）四种果品仍然是现代中式婚礼中的必需品。

90.Wedding customs

Generally speaking, traditional wedding customs in Han nationality is representative of Chinese wedding customs, which consist of 7 essential steps: matchmaking, engagement, betrothal gift, to marry, weddings (three bows), drinking wedlock wine, and the bridal chamber. Derived from the cultural accumulation of several thousand years, almost all customs in traditional weddings reflect the traditional philosophy of Chinese people, some of which have been forgotten or have been neglected by modern people, but the spirit has been affecting people more or less. For example, red color, symbolizing good wishes and happiness in Chinese culture, is still carried on in modern wedding, where the bride must wear red gown and red shoes, and the room must be decorated with red shuangxi, and new couples must have red quits. Four stuffs must be sprinkled in the bed of the new couple: dates, peanuts, longans, lotus seeds, which represent new couples have a baby as soon as possible in Chinese culture.

91. 二十四节气

根据自然的变化，将一年分成二十四个节气，这是我们祖先订立的一种用来指导农事的历法。从立春到夏至，从小暑到大寒，自然界的荣枯变化无不与太阳密切相关。因为农事基本围绕太阳进行，所以二十四节气是单独反映太阳运行周期的历法。作为中国农历中的一个重要组成部分，二十四节气反映了人们对大自然的敬畏，以及希望与大自然和谐相处的良好意愿。在传统的养生观中，人们也根据不同的节气，对身体做出不同的调理，以期达到人与自然的和谐。

91.The 24 Solar Terms

According to the changes of nature, early Chinese divided a year into 24 solar terms, which can be used to guide farming. From the Start of Spring, to the Summer Solstice, from Minor Heat to Major Cold, the waxing and waning of the nature is closely related to the sun. Since farming is changed with the sun, the 24 solar terms is a supplementary calendar based on the movements of the sun. As an essential part of Chinese lunar calendar, 24 solar terms reflect the reverence people held for nature, and their best wishes to keep in harmony with nature. In the traditional concept of preserving health, Chinese people make a different way to nurse their physical bodies, according to the diverse terms, to achieve the harmony of man and nature.

92. 十二生肖

十二生肖是中国及东亚地区的一些民族用来代表年份的十二种动物。十二生肖按固定的顺序排列，每十二年重复一次。中国的十二生肖分别是：鼠、牛、虎、兔、龙、蛇、马、羊、猴、鸡、狗、猪。这十二种动物中，除了龙之外，其余全是生活中真实能见的动物。这些生肖纪年通俗而且方便，所以中国人历来十分看重生肖，甚至认为生肖与性格、命运紧密相连，正是因为这一点，生肖成为中国久传不衰的民俗文化之一。

92.12 Chinese Zodiacs

The 12 zodiacs, consisting of 12 animals which represent a

cyclical concept of time, are used by Chinese and Some other East Asians. The 12 animal signs followed one by one in an established order, and repeated every 12 years. Chinese Zodiac animals are listed as following: the rat, the ox, the tiger, the rabbit, the Loong, the snake, the horse, the sheep, the monkey, the rooster, the dog, and the pig. They are all real animals except the loong. Due to the popularity and convenience of Zodiac calendar, Chinese has always taken it seriously, even think it is closely related to one's personality and fate, for which Chinese zodiac become one of the long-live folk cultures of China.

93. 四大发明

指南针、火药、造纸术、印刷术是闻名世界的中国四大发明，在人类文明史上有着重要的地位。

指南针的前身叫司南，是古代劳动人民发明的一种辨别方向的简易装置，11 世纪时演变成了现在的指南针。指南针的发明对世界航海事业的发展做出了伟大贡献。

火药的发明有一定的偶然性，它是中国古代炼丹家们炼制长生不老药的结果，但发明者对它并不感兴趣，它的配方由炼丹家转到军事家手里，就成为中国古代四大发明之一，在战场上发挥着巨大的作用。

纸是中国劳动人民长期经验的积累和智慧的结晶，但西汉之前的纸质地粗糙，成本高，不普及。直到经过东汉时期蔡伦的改进，才形成了一套较为定型的造纸工艺流程。造纸术的发明和推广，对于世界科学、文化的传播产生了深刻的影响。

印刷术开始于隋朝（581—618）的雕版印刷，经宋朝人毕昇（970—1051）的发展、完善，产生了活字印刷，并由蒙古人传至欧洲。印刷术为知识的广泛传播、交流创造了条件。

93.The Four Great Inventions

The compass, gunpowder, paper making, and printing are well-known in the world as the four great inventions of China. They played an important role in the history of human civilization.

Sinan, the forerunner of compass, is a device that ancient Chinese created for telling direction, which was developed into compass in the 11th century. The invention of compass contributed a lot to the development of navigation of the whole world.

The birth of gunpowder was quite accidental in some degree. It was first invented inadvertently by alchemists while attempting to make the elixir of immorality. But the inventor showed no interest in it. When taken by militarists, it became one of the four great inventions in China, and played a big part in wars.

The invention of papermaking derived from a long-term accumulation of experience, showing the wisdom of Chinese people, but for a long time it was not popular with high cost and rough quality. It didn't form a relatively stereotyped papermaking process until Cai

Lun in Eastern Han Dynasty improved it. The invention and promotion of papermaking have a profound impact on the spread of science and culture in the world.

Printing technique started with the woodblock printing in Sui Dynasty(A.D. 581-618). Improved and refined by Bi Sheng（A.D. 970-1051） in Song Dynasty, typography appeared and spread by the Mongols to Europe. Typography has contributed a lot to the wide-spread and exchange of knowledge.

第四部分 翻译练习

把下面短文翻译成英语或汉语：

94. 姓氏文化

姓氏是代表每个人及其家族的一种符号。中国姓氏的起源可以追溯到远古的母系氏族制时期。当时人们都随母姓，作为区分氏族部落的特定标志符号，因此中国的许多古代姓都是女字旁，表示女人所生。后来，部落子孙繁荣，同一“姓”中分支出不同的“氏”。“氏”后来又渐渐成为有地位的男人的称号。如中国的远古祖先黄帝本姓“姬”，后来继承神农为王，便称为“轩辕氏”。到秦汉时期，“姓”和“氏”的含义逐渐合一，统称为“姓”，是有共同父亲血缘关系的家庭称号。现在中国人的姓，大部分是代代相传下来的。有人统计，文献记载和现存的姓共有5 600多个。后世之姓，大约有以下几种来源：以氏、国名、邑名、乡或亭名、居住地、动植物或图腾等为姓，如吴、东郭、马、李等；以先人的字或名、排行、官职、技艺或职业、谥号为姓，如上官、陶等；古代少数民族融合到汉族中带来的姓；因赐姓、避讳而改姓。

95. 禁忌文化

中国普遍有“好事成双”的说法，因而凡是大贺大喜之事，所送之礼，均好双忌单。但人们忌讳“4”这个偶数，因为在汉语中，“4”听起来就像“死”，是不吉利的。再如，白色虽有纯洁无瑕之意，但中国人比较忌讳，因为在中国，白色常是大悲之色和贫穷之色。同样，黑色也被视为不吉利，是凶灾之色、哀丧之色。另外，我国人民还常常讲究给老人不能送钟，给夫妻或情人不能送梨，因“送钟”与“送终”，“梨”与“离”谐音，是不吉利的。还有，如不能为健康人送药品，不能为异性朋友送贴身的用品等。据说领带和腰带是不宜送给男性的，除非你和他有亲密关系。因为这些东西有要拴住对方的意思。依此类推，送女性项链好像也不太合适，更不用说戒指了。当然，随着中西方文化的相互交流和渗透，有些传统的禁忌也逐渐被打破，如白色尤其在拍摄婚纱照时就受到新人们的热捧，在热闹的婚礼上见到身穿白色婚纱的新娘也就不足为奇了。

96. Lucky numbers

As a key part of Chinese culture, lucky numbers draw much attention. Certain numbers, refined from the long-term daily life, are believed to be auspicious or inauspicious because their pronunciations sound similar to certain words that have lucky or unlucky meanings. For example, common people believe that even numbers can bring good luck as influenced by the saying “good things should be in pair”. Therefore, people often select lucky numbers when choosing residences, telephone numbers, business addresses, wedding dates, festivals and other celebratory events.

The numbers 3, 6, 8, and 9, though some odd numbers, are considered as lucky because their pronunciations are similar to words that have positive meanings. Specifically, the number 6 and 9 pronounced as “liu” and “jiu”, quite resembling to the words “fluid” and “long-lasting” respectively in Chinese, conveys indirectly its homophony's meaning–the former means everything goes smoothly while the latter refers to having a happy and long life, which are often used in business, work and weddings. Number 3 and 8, as they sound like “sheng” and “fa” in Cantonese, which stand for “alive” and “prosperity” or “making a fortune” separately. All businessmen favor these numbers very much.

97. Face Culture

“Face” (mianzi) is a unique cultural and psychological phenomenon of the Chinese, which has greatly influenced the Chinese daily life. A lot of foreigners can't understand why the Chinese arc so concerned about face-saving. Actually, it is impossible to figure out many Chinese behaviors without the insights into face culture in China. Face is what the Chinese are mostly concerned about. We Chinese are all too familiar with the concepts of having face, giving face and losing face,etc. The concept of face can be generally described as someone's social status or reputation in the eyes of others. In Chinese culture, if someone has good face, such face means someone has a good reputation in front of one's peers. Chinese parents tend to think their child earns them a lot of face when the child is academically successful, while they think their child makes them lose face when the child has poor academic performance. To save face, someone even may say or do what is contrary to his true intention on some occasions. However, at present, Chinese face culture, to a great extent, has become the fetters of people striving for seeking truth and making innovation. For fear of losing face, people do not dare to try new things, they lose the courage to overcome the difficulty; to maintain the so-called face or identity, people don't want to assume responsibility for their mistakes. All that we should abandon is the negative aspects in face culture.

第五部分 练习参考译文

94. Surname Culture

Surname is the sign for someone and his family. The origin of Chinese surnames can be traced back to the ancient matriarchal society in which the mother's surname, as a specific mark to identify and distinguish tribes, would be inherited. Therefore, the character for surname is formed by combining the characters for "female", which simply means "given birth by a woman". Later as the tribal society expended, different "lineages" branched out from the same surname. The hereditary lineage gradually became the title for man of status. One example is the earliest ancestral forebear of all Chinese people, the Yellow Emperor from antiquity, whose original surname was Ji, but he subsequently assumed the "Xuan Yuan Lineage" after inheriting the throne from Shen Nong. By the Qin and Han periods, the distinction between "surname" and "lineage" gradually blurred and were eventually combined into a single surname, which became the family name for kinsman related by blood and sharing the same birth father.

Most of the Chinese surnames are inherited from generation to generation through a long time. According to the statistics, there are totally 5,600 surnames in documentary and in use today. Generally,

Chinese surnames are derived from the lineage, the country, the fiefdom, village, the living place, plant, animal or totem, such as Wu, Dongguo, Ma, and Li, etc. Some of them may come from the personal names of the ancestors, the seniority among brothers and sisters, the official position, the skill or occupation, and the posthumous title. Some are brought in by the ancient minorities or granted by the emperors or changed for the taboo.

95. Taboos

There is a saying in China that "good things should be in pair". Therefore, on any happy occasion, the gifts should be sent in pair, not in single. But Number 4 is considered as a taboo and unlucky for it sounds like "dead" in Chinese. Another example is white color, which is associated with sadness and poverty in China despite of its connotation of purity. Likewise, black is also believed to be unlucky and reminds people of disaster and funeral. In China, you should devote particular care to avoid sending clock to elder people because in Chinese the character "钟" (clock) pronounces like the other character "终" (burial). For couples or lovers, you cannot send pear, which is a homophone for the word "separate". Moreover, medicine isn't a suitable gift for healthy person and personal products such as tie and belt are considered inappropriate for male friends unless you have a very intimate relationship with him, because they have a special meaning of strengthen the bonds between you and your male friend. For a female friend, you should be careful to avoid sending necklace, let alone ring. With the exchanges and penetrations between Chinese and the western culture, some traditional taboos have been broken. An example is the color of white which has prevailed among young couples when taking their wedding photos. It is no wonder that you can see the bride wear the white wedding gown in a hot wedding.

参考资料及文献

[1] 王佐良 . 英语文体学论文集 [C]. 北京 : 外语教学与研究出版社 ,1980.

[2] 赵萱 , 郑仰成 . 英汉科技翻译 [M]. 北京 : 外语教学与研究出版社 ,2006.

[3] 郑绍棠 . 新视野大学英语 [M]. 北京 : 外语教学与研究出版社 ,2011.

[4] 百度百科 . http://baike.baidu.com/ 2013.12-2014.2.

[5] 百度图片 . http://image.baidu.com/i?tn=baiduimage&ct=201326592&lm.

[6] 中国文化网 http://www.chinaculture.org/.

[7] http://www.nipic.com/show/.